Women and Problem Gambling

Addiction is much misunderstood. Women and addictive gambling even more so, and for many years women have suffered in silence. This book explores how lonely, troubled lives and damaging relationships can lead to the trap of problem gambling, and the anxiety and chaos while locked inside; it then offers realistic hope of a way out.

With the significant increase in women gambling problematically, as reported by the British Gambling Prevalence Survey (Gambling Commission, 2010), *Women and Problem Gambling* aims to answer the often asked question, 'Who is to blame?'

The text covers:

- the role of the gambling industry
- the role of society
- women's relationships with others and themselves
- what 'hitting rock bottom' truly is.

Case studies illustrate how gambling begins as harmless escapism, and how stressful and sometimes painful lives, combined with spiralling debts, can lead to desperation to avoid thoughts, feelings and the reality of life in chaos. Women can, and do, stop gambling – in this book Liz Karter shares anecdotes from clients and discusses therapeutic models and practical strategies to demonstrate how this is possible.

Women and Problem Gambling is based on the author's research and theories developed throughout her extensive practice. The insights will be of value to anyone wanting to understand or work with problem gambling in women; from a woman with a problem herself, through to family, friends and any healthcare professionals or therapists involved in her care and treatment.

Liz Karter rking exclusively in the field of prot

Women and Problem Gambling

Therapeutic insights into understanding addiction and treatment

Liz Karter

Routledge
Taylor & Francis Group

LONDON AND NEW YORK

First published 2013
by Routledge
27 Church Road, Hove, East Sussex BN3 2FA

Simultaneously published in the USA and Canada
by Routledge
711 Third Avenue, New York, NY 10017

Routledge is an imprint of the Taylor & Francis Group, an informa business

British Library Cataloguing in Publication Data
A catalogue record for this book is available from the British Library

Library of Congress Cataloging-in-Publication Data
Karter, Elizabeth, 1966–
   Women and problem gambling : therapeutic insights into
   understanding addiction and treatment / Elizabeth Karter.
      p. cm.
   Includes bibliographical references and index.
1. Women gamblers. 2. Compulsive gambling. I. Title.
HV6710.K37 2013
616.85'84106082–dc23   20120388

ISBN: 978–0–415–68636–5 (hbk)
ISBN: 978–0–415–68637–2 (pbk)
ISBN: 978–0–203–56543–8 (ebk)

Typeset in Times New Roman
by Swales & Willis Ltd, Exeter, Devon

MIX
Paper from
responsible sources
FSC® C013056
www.fsc.org

Printed and bound in Great Britain by
TJ International Ltd, Padstow, Cornwall

For my mother, Avril. And for Hannah, Benjamin and Jessica. For years of 'team work'.

Contents

Preface

Women and Problem Gambling wanted to be written, or certainly it appears so, and has been in the process of being written for the last ten years. I say this because I have been fortunate to work exclusively in the field of problem gambling throughout that time. Much of the theory and practice I describe in this book has developed organically, resulting from my working extensively with women who gamble problematically. This process has taught me what led to their being lost in problem gambling, and what it is that best 'works' therapeutically, to enable them to find a way out.

In truth, I wonder if mental notes for this book started to be taken even before I had the ability to write, when as a child I spent time in puzzled awe on the outer circle of the group made up of my mother and women of my extended family, who would regularly meet at my grandmother's house. Now, on reflection, I understand that what they were doing was so much more than what seemed to me to be having endless pots of tea and dull chat. What they were doing (whether their conscious intention or not) was benefiting from this ritual in terms of coming together for support and healthy emotional expression. This, too, was the beginning of my developing understanding of the value in the telling of, and the listening to, stories of our life experience, and that of our ancestors, as a way of better understanding ourselves, and why we are where we are, and why we are who we are, in our here and now lives.

I feel I have been blessed in that the opportunities that have arisen throughout my career, and the choices I have made, have all led to the compilation of material for this book being a naturally flowing process. All that I have then needed to do is capture, and get down on paper, the essence of the women, their lives, situations and gambling patterns, which have been a part of the many rich, varied and rewarding therapeutic relationships that have shaped my therapeutic practice.

On first beginning my career as a counsellor and psychotherapist, I took a placement with a voluntary organisation specialising in work with the adult survivors of abuse and rape, and I wrote my thesis on abuse-related trauma. A year later, I began work as a problem gambling therapist with GamCare, one of the leading agencies in the UK. It was soon apparent that the skills I had learnt, working with trauma, would often be called on in my work with problem gambling, both with men and women.

Six years ago, noticing the difference in the patterns of gambling behaviour in men and women, and believing the need for this to be recognised in treatment, I established for GamCare the first UK group exclusively for women with problem gambling issues, and found the outcomes highly successful. I went on to establish and facilitate these groups for other UK problem gambling treatment agencies, including Breakeven and the National Problem Gambling Clinic, and in my own private practice, Level Ground Therapy, which I established to meet the needs of women with gambling problems and related issues.

Frequent opportunities began to arise to write and to speak about my work, in newsprint, television and radio broadcast. When invited by Routledge to write *Women and Problem Gambling*, I was delighted. An issue that so often leads to women developing gambling problems is feeling silenced. They are afraid to voice their emotional and psychological distress. Many of the women I am working with currently in treatment, or have worked with during the process of writing *Women and Problem Gambling* have known about the coming publication. I have received nothing but encouragement (and I would like to acknowledge this same enthusiastic response to the book from my male clients). The women have told me that they are only too pleased for their voices to be heard – not only for reasons of creating greater understanding of their own battles with problem gambling, but also that other women might be encouraged to come forward to seek help.

I have chosen to write this book in the same style in which I speak and write generally about my work: in 'layman's terms', using plain English instead of therapeutic terminology. This is because I wish *Women and Problem Gambling* to be accessible to all who might have an interest – be it professional or personal – in the increasingly high-profile issue of women and problem gambling. Over the years, during conversations with social workers, probation officers and mental health workers, I have found them all keen to help the women they engage with through their services, but frequently at a loss to understand the underlying motivation for problematic gambling behaviour.

Many women for whom gambling is out of control find it hard to explain to those close to them how it feels to be locked into problem gambling, and I have sometimes been asked if I will speak to family members and partners on their behalf – to be their voice. I am honoured to have the opportunity to do so now, through this book.

Acknowledgements

My family have been a constant reminder of what is most important in life, and I appreciate their understanding of my frequent unavailability and preoccupation during the writing of *Women and Problem Gambling*. I thank you for your love and support.

My friends, and 'train friends'. All have given me invaluable encouragement and motivation, and a listening ear.

With groups of both friends and family, I am so very fortunate to be a part of such a strong support network.

I would like to thank my colleagues, many of whom I would also call friends, for their inspiring confidence in my ability to write this book.

Of course, thank you so much to all of the women who, both in groups and individually, have shared their stories, enabling *Women and Problem Gambling* to make sense, take shape and come to life. Thank you too, for your enthusiastic response to the concept of this book.

Finally and importantly, I wish to thank the men who are clients within my practice, who showed support for, and interest in, this project.

Acknowledgements

Chapter 1

Growing the problem

If we read newspapers and magazines, if we watch television or listen to the radio, we do not now have to try very hard to come across a subject that until recently was relatively unheard of: that of women with gambling addiction. We read sensational stories of women heavily in debt, children neglected, theft committed and even prison sentences served. We read the surface story perhaps with dark interest and confusion as to how the woman could allow herself to get into such a dire situation. Some ask incredulously, 'Why doesn't she *just stop gambling*?' In the first chapter of this book we will begin to read between the lines, and to understand that there is a story behind the media accounts we now hear with increasing frequency.

In the ten years in which I have been practising as a psychotherapist working exclusively in the field of problem gambling, with all its related issues, I have always known that many women have gambled socially and, if they can gamble socially, they can of course gamble problematically. Anything we do that we enjoy, and is recreational and pleasurable, ultimately has that potential to get a little out of hand. It is after all a part of our human nature that if something makes us feel good we want to repeat the experience.

Those of us who gamble socially do so for various reasons but primarily for reasons of entertainment. For some, it is because we enjoy the excitement associated with the activity, lifting us out of what can be mundane day-to-day life. Others of us might like to challenge ourselves mentally, trying to work out a system, developing skills to try to beat the odds. We can also experience a sense of relaxation when gambling – focusing on something that absorbs us to the extent that we are not thinking about our life problems for a while. We enjoy switching off from stresses and anxieties.

In a health and safety conscious culture where we are urged to be cautious at all times, it is easy to forget that it can be fun and healthy, if not essential to our overall well-being to take a little risk. Gambling offers us an element of risk.

Whatever our own particular experience, if we are social or regular gamblers, the activity offers us a form of entertainment and therefore, as with all forms of entertainment, an element of escapism. For the majority of the population, gambling is just a good source of fun .

The third British Gambling Prevalence Survey (BGPS) 2010 built on the two previous gambling prevalence surveys published in 2000 and 2007. The key aims of the BGPS were to:

- measure prevalence of participation in all forms of commercial and private gambling;
- estimate prevalence of problem gambling;
- investigate sociodemographic factors associated with problem gambling;
- explore attitudes to gambling;
- provide comparisons between pre- and post-implementation of the Gambling Act 2005 (Gambling Commission, 2010).

The survey found that nearly three-quarters (73 per cent) of adults in Britain gambled (rising from 68 per cent in 2007), the vast majority saying they gambled for fun and the chance of winning money.

The proportion of problem gamblers increased from 0.5 per cent of the adult population in 2007 to 0.7 per cent in 2010, and the BGPS (2010) indicated a significant rise in female problem gambling from 0.2 per cent in 2007 to 0.3 per cent in 2010 .

Most of us keep a healthy balance between the things that make us feel good and offer escapism, and our day-to-day responsibilities. It is only when that balance tips that problems start, and we may develop what is termed an addiction, a dependency or a problem. Depending on clinical background and preferred model of problem gambling treatment, there will be a 'label of choice' to refer to problem gambling. For the purpose of this book, and not wishing to get bogged down in debating terminology, I will use the term 'problem gambling' to cover the spectrum of gambling activity that is recognised as out-of-control behaviour.

So, what is it that has caused the balance to tip from social or regular gambling to problem or pathological gambling for so many more women in the last few years? The media is one area that has been whipped into a frenzy of curiosity as to what has caused this sudden phenomenon.

In my role specialising in women and problem gambling, I have many times been asked by the media to comment on whether:

1. I think that the gambling industry has cleverly used an advertising campaign to 'lure' women into a gambling habit;
2. I think the gambling industry is causing a vulnerable group to develop problems.

To the first question I tend to answer that I think yes, clearly the gambling industry has launched an advertising campaign aimed at women because there is now such a vast range of female-friendly products that they are promoting. The gambling industry is an entertainment industry and its intention is to promote its business, as any other business might.

In answer to the second question, I think that women are as vulnerable to advertisements for gambling as they are to advertisements for alcohol, cigarettes, comfort food and shopping . . . whatever is pleasurable and offers a little time out from day-to-day life. That does not mean to say that every woman who plays a game of bingo online will inevitably become a problem gambler, any more than a woman who has a glass of alcohol that is sold as particularly attractive to her gender will become an alcoholic, or the woman who buys a tub of seductively marketed ice cream will develop an addiction to comfort eating. However, in all these areas some women will develop problems and professional experience has taught me that the woman who develops a problem does so because she had what she feels to be intolerable life problems anyway. The reasons women develop gambling problems are much more complex than just being attracted like moths to a flame of advertising, as we shall explore. Gambling becomes out of control often as a response to feeling psychologically overwhelmed and emotionally out of control.

The advertising of gambling products that appeal to women, and the advertising of gambling activities in general, have increased. The Gambling Act 2005, which came into effect in 2007, allowed the responsible advertising of gambling, and, for the first time, introduced licensing of online gambling (Gambling Commission, 2005).

There is as yet no statistical evidence to support the notion that there has been a rise in online gambling since 2007. Online gambling has, however, been the focus of media speculation as to whether it is a cause of more women than ever before being attracted to gambling and therefore potentially developing problems. Glamorously glossy advertisements invite women to try out new games that they might never have played before in the privacy of their own homes, and away from any embarrassment of learning to play an unfamiliar game in front of more experienced gamblers in a land-based casino.

> The latest Commerce and Online Gaming Regulation and Assurance (eCogra) study of almost 11,000 online players from 96 countries found the average online casino player was female with 54.8 per cent of online casino games players women (eCogra, 2010).

Online bingo sites send a digital invitation for a night out with the girls – without having to make the effort of choosing an outfit, leaving the home in the cold and the dark, attending a venue alone and meeting new people – to women whose social lives may be lacking.

Online gambling has attracted a younger female player, perhaps because of the ease with which younger people use digital technology as a part of day-to-day life. It is now even possible to gamble on a smartphone, making gambling available 24 hours a day.

> In July 2011 the RCA Trust logged a 15 per cent increase in women of all ages getting into debt through internet poker and bingo sites. (Caernarfon Denbigh Herald, 2011).

In recent years, the image of more established forms of gambling has undergone a dramatic makeover too. Land-based bingo halls are no longer perceived as the exclusive domain of senior citizens. Modern advertising has attracted a younger female clientele, who now view bingo as a fun night out with the girls.

> Rank Group, owners of Mecca Bingo, reported a 40 per cent increase in under-35s playing bingo (Thomas, 2012).

The bookmakers' shops of the past conjured images of smoke-filled 'dens of iniquity', a very male territory, the interior of which most women might only imagine, as few would dare, or wish, to venture inside. Nowadays, bookmakers are permitted to open shops in prominent positions on the high street. Gone are the covered windows concealing uninviting, dingy rooms. We can look in on brightly lit spaces, decorated in the familiar colours of fast-food restaurants, where we can sit comfortably over coffee, if we so wish. Fixed Odds Betting Terminals, reminiscent in appearance of traditional slot machines, offer us digital casino games if we are not tempted to place traditional bets.

Casinos traditionally trigger the image of James Bond, the stereotypical 'alpha male', with the only place for a woman in the casino perhaps on his arm, standing like 'Lady Luck' at his side. Women now go to a casino for a night out with friends or dinner with a partner, and they have become much more comfortable with being an active participant in playing table games and slot machines.

Horse racing . . . Almost every significant race meeting on the calendar now advertises its 'Ladies' Day' via radio and newsprint. The invitation to dress glamorously, wear a hat, drink a glass or two of champagne amid stunning countryside views is appealing enough in itself. Add to that the thrill of watching magnificent animals race to the finish with maybe the added excitement of having a little money on the race. It is no wonder now that it is not at all unusual to see parties exclusively of women attending race meetings, for a day out.

Even an evening at the dog track no longer has the image of men in cloth caps standing in the drizzling rain, but is now potentially a more polished social event – an evening out to dinner with the option of placing bets without needing to leave your table.

Slot machine arcades have traditionally had a family-friendly, seaside holiday image. Tea and coffee are offered to regular customers, greeted as friends. We will explore both the environment of the amusement arcade, and the world of online gambling in more detail in later chapters.

So we can see that gambling as a recreational activity and a social event has become increasingly appealing to, and normalised for, women. Perhaps this process of the increase in social gambling for women really began with the advent of the UK National Lottery in 1994 (BBC, 1994). Suddenly, advertising began to normalise gambling, people who had never gambled before bought tickets and gambling began to be socially acceptable. After all, buying a lottery ticket at the supermarket suddenly cut out the stigma attached to being a woman who gambles. So too, when in 1995 scratchcards were launched (National Lottery, 2012). What could feel more normal and socially acceptable than doing the weekly super-market shop? Therefore, if we pick up our scratchcards along with our trolley full of groceries, perhaps that makes the process an even more acceptable part of day-to-day living. Advertisements for online gambling sites viewed before our favourite TV soap again give the sense of gambling being an established part of everyday life. What can feel more reassuringly established than the soap we have watched on the same day, at the same time, for years?

It might seem that, having said that I do not lay blame at the door of the gambling industry, I am now contradicting myself by giving evidence for the way in which women have been tempted into problem gambling. That is not what I am attempting to prove. What I aim to show is that gambling has been made more accessible to women and more fun for women, and that for the majority of women who enjoy gambling as entertainment and a bit of healthy escapism, that is absolutely okay.

To one extent or another we all use something to escape the pressures of day-to-day life, or sometimes perhaps to avoid being bothered by uncomfortable thoughts and feelings from our past or present: a stressful job or a painful relationship break-up, for example. Whether we read a book, watch a film, play a video game or go to the theatre, these are all ways of escape into another world where for a time it feels like nothing else matters. In healthy circumstances, after some time out we then re-enter our 'real world' to pick up our responsibilities, and we feel refreshed and better able to manage. Gambling will not become a problem for women who can use the escape that it offers healthily and in balance in this way. Contemporary life is hard at times. We have to work harder to keep our balance, and not favour escape over whatever is our 'real life'.

The desire many women have to escape elements of modern Western society can in part be measured by the popularity of the book, and the film of the book *Eat, Pray, Love*, based on the real life experiences of the author Elizabeth Gilbert. We watch the lead character, Liz, becoming painfully conscious that the life she has been an active participant in creating does not feel authentically hers. She feels she is merely a physical presence in her marriage and is tired of feeling soulless and joyless, no longer alive but merely existing. She is tired of feeling guilt at the things that might bring her small delights, such as the pleasure of eating, because she has swallowed whole the Western obsession with physical perfection. She somehow finds the courage within herself to literally escape from her life, leaving the security of her marriage and home, and a successful career, to embark on a journey of self-discovery, finding authentic friendships and falling in love with life; learning the meaning of true intimacy in a new romantic relationship (Gilbert, 2006).

We watched Liz and were touched by her story, because perhaps her pain and frustration resonated with our own. We felt maybe similar desires within us to tear up the material of unsatisfactory lives, which somehow we had created, but now felt stuck in. We admired her courage and understood her procrastination because we know deep within us the scariness of leaving what we know, however dysfunctional it may be, just because it is what we know, and with it we feel safe. If we make a change, we do not know what will happen, and not knowing can be frightening. So Liz, and her experience, is a metaphor for the experience of so many women. Metaphor feels safe because it is one removed from ourselves. We can watch and feel and think, but not actively participate and *risk* any negative consequences. Some of us of course were perhaps so inspired by the film and other such stories, either true or fictional, that we did make the break for freedom, or at least make adjustments in life so that we felt a little less trapped, a little more like ourselves.

In the film, Liz, clearly, is relatively lucky. She has an independent financial income, no dependent children, a good support network of friends, physical health and comparative youth on her side.

What happens to the women who feel they cannot make the break for freedom? Who watch Liz and hear a quiet voice inside them begin to say 'That's me, that's how I feel', but do not, or feel they cannot, vacate their own lives, perhaps because they do not have enough money, they have too many responsibilities and others depending on them, or they do not have the physical strength as a result of chronic illness. Some may feel they do not yet have the emotional resources, or have good reason to be afraid for their safety if they took the risk. Those women hear the voice inside them getting louder and louder telling them 'This is not what I wanted for my life', 'This is all too much, I'm exhausted' until they end up silently screaming in the life in which they now feel trapped. They find a way to silence the voice when listening to it creates feelings that are just too painful. Some silence the voice by having another couple of glasses of wine, smoking a few more cigarettes, eating some more chocolate bars, pushing a few more coins into a fruit machine or switching on the computer and focusing on playing a game for a while – maybe a while too long; maybe buying a few more scratchcards than they can afford in the hope that a big win might be life changing. In extreme cases, they find themselves craving more and more of the escape they find in whatever way they find it, and less and less of real life. And that, in the simplest of terms, is how a gambling problem, a dependency, an addiction starts.

Addiction treatment agencies see the results of women who have the desire to escape, but do not, or feel they cannot, literally vacate or make adjustments in the problematic areas of their life. Many drug and alcohol treatment agencies have recently issued reports indicating that more and more women are coming forward seeking treatment for drug and alcohol problems. So, should we then really be surprised at the fact that there is an increase in women who have gambling problems too?

In February 2011 the Gambling Commission released the results of its latest prevalence survey into problem gambling in the British population. The survey had been conducted in 2010 using random samples of British households. All members of the selected household aged 18 years or above were asked to complete the *Diagnostic and Statistical Manual of Mental Disorders (DSM)* problem gambling screen (American Psychiatric Association, 2000) using a laptop computer. The sample totalled 7,756 individuals.

The main findings of the 2010 problem gambling survey were as follows:

- Six per cent of the population of Great Britain were problem gamblers.
- Male problem gambling had increased from 10 per cent in 2007 to 15 per cent in 2010.
- Female problem gambling had increased from 0.2 per cent in 2007 to 0.3 per cent in 2010. This translates to 75,000 women in Great Britain (Gambling Commission, 2010).

My professional opinion on these figures for female problem gambling is that this is the tip of the iceberg.

Throughout the length of my practice, almost every one of the many women I have worked with in treatment has commented on the fact that she is surprised that I, or the agencies I have worked with, are not inundated with women seeking help for problem gambling, because these women know how many others are out there. They of course recognise the signs. Historically, as mentioned earlier, the vast majority of women who have gambled problematically have been slot machine players. So much was this the pattern that I came to predict that every woman, at her assessment for treatment, would describe slot machines as her problematic mode of gambling. The signs of problematic slot machine playing are easy for others to spot. These include total focus on the machine, relentless feeding of the machine with coins until there are no coins left, frustration and desperation visibly present when play has to stop, and long periods absent from home or work to engage in the activity.

The advent of online gambling made problem gambling a lot harder to identify. The signs may be similar but are much easier to hide. The woman with an online gambling problem can play alone at home – away from eyes that might identify signs very similar to those shown by women whose slot machine playing has become out of control. Absence from home or work is no longer an issue; as long as the computer screen is hidden, so is the gambling problem.

As highlighted earlier in this chapter, the arrival of online gambling and its advertising campaign had, and still has, the media buzzing with the idea that women gamble. The topic has featured in broadcast media, newsprint and magazines, and as a result women are beginning to feel that the subject of being a woman who gambles to excess is now a *little* less taboo than previously so. In one sense, the availability of online gambling potentially enables a woman's gambling problem to remain concealed for longer; in another sense, I wonder if the high-profile association it has with women gambling has been a catalyst for more women finding the courage to admit to themselves and to others that they have a gambling problem.

Historically women have found it incredibly hard to approach treatment. When I first began to practise in this field, it was a very rare moment indeed when a woman would approach the problem gambling treatment agencies I worked for. If one did come forward, she would often be convinced that she was the only woman who had ever had a gambling problem. As discussed, gambling has been perceived until now as a primarily male recreational activity, and certainly a very male addiction. The woman coming forward to ask for help has double the difficulties in terms of emotional, psychological and social blocks to doing so: not only does she have an addiction problem, she is a *woman* who has an addiction problem, to what is perceived as a male-dominated behaviour. We shall explore the area of difficulty in engaging women in treatment in more depth in later chapters of this book.

So, an increasingly high proportion of women are aware that problem gambling is a very real issue, and that problem gambling is an issue for women too. As a result, they are feeling more confident about coming forward to say that they have a problem, and want and need support. That has to be a good thing. Perhaps then, what we are seeing in the results of the gambling prevalence study is not necessarily so much of a rise in the actual numbers of women gambling, but a rise in the numbers of women who are able to identify and acknowledge a problem in their own behaviour? That I think is for consideration. What about the fact, however, that there is an increase in numbers of women with addiction problems reported by other addiction agencies?

It could be true of course that women with addictions to alcohol and drugs, and those with eating disorders, are also feeling more okay about saying, 'I have a problem and I need help.' Perhaps there is an element of this behaviour. With high-profile celebrities publishing stories of meltdown and rehab clinics, one argument is that it has possibly become not only less taboo but almost fashionable in some areas of society to have an addiction. That does not, however, fit with my experience of most women with addiction. Addiction in almost all women who gamble problematically is truly a dependency. They *depend* on their gambling, because on some level their experience is that it helps to get them through life. It is an attempt to cope with what feels emotionally and psychologically overwhelming and intolerable – an attempt to cope by escaping for a while, but then finding they cannot come back: they have just created another trap.

Women in contemporary Western society have many good reasons to need an escape route at times. We have been exploring the impact of gambling industry advertising in terms of influencing potentially vulnerable women, but we are flooded every day with advertisements of an equally, if not more, dangerous kind. They instil a message in us that in order to feel okay about ourselves we must own this particular home, drive this kind of car, have the designer kitchen and a hot tub in the garden. Not only is it subtly suggested to us that we should own the latest designer clothes, but a designer body too. We should strive toward attaining a state of physical perfection that is rarely achievable without use of an airbrush, and, if we cannot achieve these things naturally, not to worry – we can always purchase them.

We read about all of these 'must have' purchases, which we are told will make us fulfilled at a time when the world is in financial recession and all but the wealthiest of us struggle.

In February 2011, Asda noted that scratchcard sales had risen since the height of the financial crisis. The group said this was something that they noticed happens at a time of customer anxiety about the future (Wood, 2011).

Another bind is that, while striving to reach these material and physical goals, women should not admit openly to wanting these things because they should also always be working to prove themselves intellectually admirable by being beyond such frivolous desires. A difficulty in finding an authentic identity is a big issue for many women currently. It is of course okay to want to have or achieve any of the purchases or personal aspirations referred to earlier if we feel it is truly our free choice and we are not merely fulfilling a blind process. If we are unsure of who we truly are, what we really want, how can we possibly know what it is that is likely to make us content and fulfilled? Are we not much more likely to end up trapped in lives that do not truly feel like our own, and to crave that escape route?

In 2010 the NHS published statistics reporting that 20 per cent of adult women were being treated for mental health disorders. The figures for men were 12 per cent (Wilson, 2011).

I believe it is important to say at this stage that the purpose of this book is not to put forward a case that women have it hard and men have it easy. That is not my intention, because it is not what I believe. Men undoubtedly are struggling with many similar practical and identity issues. What I *do* believe is that, for biological and social reasons, men and women have different experiences of being in the world. The purpose of this book is to focus primarily on the experience of women in relation to problem gambling, and so that shall be our area of concentration.

We may live in a time when we have less to worry about on a physical and basic survival level than ever before. A time in which we have less extreme poverty than ever before; it is rare that any of us will starve, most of us expect shelter, we have eradicated most of the Dickensian-type diseases that plagued us. In modern society, the diseases that plague us most now are often those of a psychological and emotional kind:

• In 2011, Platform 51 (a women's campaign group) released results from a study indicating that one in three women had taken anti-depressants during their lifetime (Platform 51, 2011).
• Statistics taken from groups I have facilitated over the last five years, 2006–11, show that 74 per cent of group members have a diagnosed mental health problem ranging from depression or anxiety to personality disorder.

So what is it that has brought us to this point of so much psychological and emotional ill-health when surely, in the 1950s, women were in a far more restricting trap than any they may be in now? Women at that time discovered that Valium – 'mother's little helper' – was a way to quiet the screaming voice inside, and many became addicted to their medication. Perhaps what brought us to this point was in part feeling understandably so desperate to escape the trap of the stereotypical 'Stepford wife'. When we eventually got ourselves free, we maybe ran so fast that we did not stop long enough to think whether there was anything of value left there that we wanted to take with us – things such as stronger family values and traditions; men and women healthily acknowledging their differences, as well as their equality.

When as individuals we make big changes, if we are not very careful, we tend to swing pendulum-like to the opposite to what we have decided we do not want. For example, the person who has worked every day for 20 years, 9am–5pm, in the city will throw it all in to live in the middle of nowhere, only to realise that actually, on reflection, they miss the social life, or the buzz of the city that went with their job. As a society, we can do similar and maybe that is what we did when we left the 1950s 'Formica Fancy' lifestyle behind. In some ways we jumped out of the frying pan trap of our kitchens and into the fire of a confused and hugely pressured lifestyle.

It is extremely positive of course that women are out in the workplace and that, if they so wish, they may choose to have a career instead of a husband and family. But many women feel that it is not so much a choice but an expectation that they do it all, and be all things to all people, and if not they have failed. Women's magazines tell us stories of 'Wonder Women' who are juggling the demands of a successful career, happy marriage and glowing children. Conversely, we read of many women now bringing up children alone, as the stresses and strains of modern living take their toll on relationships. On the other hand, statistics released in June 2011 report that 43 per cent of generation X university-educated women remain childless (MailOnline, 2011).

Their situations may be vastly different, but loneliness and feeling emotionally isolated are often familiar experiences for each group described, and indeed many other women in today's society.

Seventy-four per cent of women's group members I have worked with live alone or alone with children.

Loneliness and isolation are often key factors for a woman falling into a gambling problem. It is in our human nature that we are social beings. We learnt to gather together as cave dwellers, knowing that we needed each other for warmth, companionship, for our very survival, relying on those stronger than ourselves to hunt and gather. We could argue of course that we have moved on so far beyond those times that there can be no possible comparison. But I think the following quote gives cause for consideration:

> For while the form of life changes, human nature does not change or only very slowly. As the Chinese *Book of Changes* says:
>
> > The Town may be changed,
> > But the well cannot be changed.
>
> . . . political structures change, as do nations, but the life of man with its needs remains eternally the same . . . (Harding, 1967: ix)

Our Town may now be unrecognisable to that of our cave-dwelling forbears; we live in comfortable houses, can order our shopping online, need never have contact with another human being if we so chose, and yet still get all our basic physical needs met. But the well of our psychological and emotional selves remains the same. We have the same need to gather together, and yet extended families now often live hundreds of miles apart, in which case we lose a source of practical help and emotional support. Inspiring and encouraging stories of how older generations came through difficult times are lost, because there is no time for the oral tradition of storytelling that is for passing down wisdom and can give us a stronger sense of identity in knowing where we came from.

Financial pressures, too much choice, too little time cause families to fragment and single parents are left to cope alone. Demanding jobs, commuting, running children to the myriad of after-school activities we are told are essential if we want to be okay parents leave us too exhausted to meet up with existing friends or to develop new ones.

If we have families and friendships, we have back-up. When life becomes so hard we feel it impossible to go on, if we can turn to another to *express* our feelings, we often get some relief. If there is no one there, and we are not just alone but lonely, we learn often to *suppress* them – to become so absorbed in the activity of feeding a slot machine, or staring at the computer screen as we play another game, engaging in the repetitive behaviour that for that time our feelings cease to exist. We are no longer bothered by our uncomfortable thoughts, and so no equally uncomfortable feelings and emotions are triggered. It is a form of self-medication.

Today, if we visit a busy GP to confide our depression or anxiety, we are likely to walk away with medication to numb our emotional pain. Close, supportive families might model that it is normal to feel depressed at, for example, a bereavement. It is normal to feel anxious at losing a job. Ideally, we would have support for our feelings while we go through them, but today's sanitised society implies we should avoid uncomfortable emotions, that we should not go through them but negotiate our way around them. Falling into gambling addiction is often an attempt to go around: to avoid going through our pain.

The popularity of Facebook and social networking sites illustrates how we all crave closeness in our busy, often isolated lives, but perhaps too, perpetuate the maintenance of distance in key relationships. If life experiences have taught us that the intimacy of a relationship is to be feared, it is very tempting to build a social life in as remote a way as possible.

Eighty-five per cent of group members have suffered abuse or domestic violence.

Later chapters will cover in the detail that these women's stories deserve the toll this has taken on their ability to trust and to be close. I am sure that even at this stage those among us reading this who have no prior knowledge of problem gambling might begin to imagine how after the ultimate betrayal of trust it feels so hard to reach out to another when we are in emotional and psychological pain. That it might just feel easier not to feel at all and so numb the feelings through a gambling activity. Or, how it might feel so impossibly lonely at times, but still much too scary to form close friendships in the 'real world', that it might feel tempting to make friends through the safety of the digital world.

A group member who had worked so hard to become and remain gambling-free, but was struggling to go out into the world and engage with others following abandonment, physical abuse and betrayal of her trust as a child, reported one week that she had gambled. The group was surprised that she had relapsed. However, what transpired was that she was not gambling for escape from uncomfortable feelings as before, but for the sense of friendship without the risk of human contact that she got from online bingo sites. She was not attracted by advertisements promising money or glamour, but the idea of friendship: of belonging to a group and no longer feeling alone.

I hope that this chapter begins to outline the possible reasons for the increase in numbers of women who gamble problematically. We have seen that it is unlikely that the increase lies solely in the increased availability and promotion of gambling, but may lie in part with the stigma and taboo of female problem gambling dissolving under the deluge of media coverage making it easier to admit to a problem.

I think what we have seen is that a key reason for an increase in female problem gambling is the problematic and often lonely society in which we now live. The most natural thing in the world is to be in relationship with others; if we have that, we have support. If we feel we do not have that support, because we have no one close, or we fear letting others close, then we are vulnerable. We are vulnerable to anything that we feel helps us to cope with, or to escape from, our most painful thoughts and feelings. Whatever the cost might be.

Chapter 2

Why take the risk?

In Chapter 1 we explored what it is that has caused a rise in the problem of women and gambling from a sociological perspective. Now, let us identify and discuss what it is that causes women to choose gambling as a coping strategy, as opposed to any other form of addiction.

The BGPS 2010, an independent report published in February 2011 by the Gambling Commission indicated that:

- nearly three-quarters of adults (73 per cent) had gambled in the previous year
- between 0.7 and 0.9 per cent (estimated 450,000) of the population have a gambling problem.
- an estimated 75,000 (0.3 per cent) of women are deemed to be problem gamblers (Gambling Commission, 2010).

Having said in the previous chapter that the focus of this book shall be on the female experience of problem gambling, it will be of value to compare the experience of women with their male counterparts, to better understand that the issue of female problem gambling has a particular set of issues requiring a particular form of treatment.

Another question that I am frequently asked, and which leads us into the theme of this chapter, is 'Is there *really* a difference in male and female problem gambling?' I fully understand this question being asked, because, when I first began to practise, I myself was not aware of the differences. Like many therapists, I understood myself to be treating a behaviour, first and foremost. My chosen therapeutic models meant that I did see addiction as having a meaning, and so I would work toward identifying the causal factors in terms of past and present life, relationships, thoughts and feelings.

It was around four years into my work, however, that I finally had a 'eureka moment'. I became aware that I had seen several clients, both male and female, who spoke of mixed-gender support groups for problem gambling, and were puzzled to hear how the opposite sex used gambling. I reflected on seeing quite different patterns in male and female gambling behaviour, and what each gender might describe as the reward from gambling. I now think it should have been obvious to me all along that, if we truly believe that addiction has a meaning, we need to identify that meaning by working with and treating not simply 'a gambler' but a *person*, and understanding where gambling fits into the context of that person's particular life. And, if we believe in working with the individual person, how can we ignore that a part of what creates individuality and meaning is gender difference? After all, men and women have different experiences of being in the world, and some experiences remain exclusive to man or woman, such as what it is to be mother or father, daughter or son. It is perceived difficulties in being in the world that create the gambling problem. The women – and men – I have worked with over the years have known themselves that there are differences, and I know it too, because they taught me.

We are, as a society, coming once again to a point of saying that it is not only okay but valuable and healthy to acknowledge gender difference, and that 'equality' does not necessarily mean 'the same as'. In other words, women and men should of course be treated as equals and have equal rights, but they do have inherent differences. So, if that is once again becoming the opinion of society, having had a largely failed and, in worst cases, damaging attempt at treating both genders the same, then surely we must give that same theory a place in addiction treatment?

One of the first aspects of difference in male and female problem gambling behaviour to come to my attention was the mode of gambling favoured by each gender. Male problem gamblers are much more likely than women to report betting as their gambling mode of choice. Betting on horse and greyhound racing, spread betting (betting on the stock exchange) on sports such as a football game are all very familiar forms reported. I have yet to come across a woman who has presented for treatment with a betting problem.

The reasons for this predominantly male choice of betting may lie in reasons we have already touched on: that historically men have had easier access than women to the bookmaker's shop, they may have seen generations of their family studying form in the newspaper and placing bets, and so they may have been socialised into betting from an early age. After all, our same-sex parent passes on to us the 'How To Guide' on thinking, feeling and behaving as a member of our gender group, and our tendency is either to adapt or to rebel against the information we receive.

Many male problem gamblers find their gambling has its roots in adapting to what they witnessed as normal male behaviour.

Often, I have heard men comment on the sense of camaraderie that they feel in the betting shop. It is a place that can be a true leveller. In such an environment it does not matter if, in life outside the shop, you are as poor as a church mouse or live the life of a king. Everyone there is there for the same purpose. It is like belonging to a select club and all that is needed to gain exclusive membership is to be a 'gambler'. For men who have a gambling problem, there can be a very real period of mourning the loss of not only their engagement with gambling but also that particular environment. And no less the social aspect of it, if their gambling problem was such that they needed to take the option of total abstinence. Often, they have needed to make the difficult choice to move on from groups of friends they have known for years, because they too are involved in the world of gambling.

The same sense of belonging is frequently described by male problem gamblers regarding the horse race track. I have heard attendance at race meetings described as 'a way of life'. It can form an essential part of the social scene for men in certain sociodemographics where, for example, business might require entertaining clients at the race track, or particular race meetings have been attended with friends and family, year in year out. The diary of significant race meetings provide a structure to the year, and plotting key events on the racing calendar are every bit as significant, and as much a part of the traditional tapestry of life, as rituals such as Christmas and birthdays.

So, I think we are beginning to see how for men who bet socially or problematically, the social aspect of their gambling is significant. The advent of online gambling and interactive TV has not changed this for some men, who may choose to avoid the bookmaker but report gathering together with others at home to gamble. This social aspect may begin to change as the problem develops and goes under cover, but, if you choose to bet in the bookmaker's shop, or on the race course, it is a very public and visible engagement with gambling. If you gamble in a betting shop or at a race course, win or lose, you are very likely to have an audience.

The idea of an audience can be appealing for some men. Placing a substantial bet, or stake at the casino table, can feel empowering. Some male clients have described enjoying the feeling of all eyes upon them in the betting shop or casino in those moments. They have imagined others perceiving them as powerful, wealthy or exciting risk takers. The reverse experience and imagined perception, of course, can be true. If the bet does not pay off, if they get hooked into loss chasing, making panic-driven attempts to win back what they have lost by placing other large bets that also do not pay off, how does it feel to have an audience then? I have found it a touching experience to work with men who have become tearful in therapy sessions as they describe feeling acutely ashamed that others must have seen them in such a desperate state, both financially and emotionally, and the fear of having been seen as 'stupid', or 'a loser' or 'weak'.

There is an equation which I identified for this dynamic:

Win = 'I am a winner' = 'I am a success'.
Lose = 'I am a loser' = 'I am a failure'.

Therefore, for male problem gamblers who are caught up in these very public types of gambling, a large part of the reward, and indeed the more punishing aspects of the behaviour, are often intrinsically linked with how they are seen by others –with their identity as a 'success' or a 'failure'.

Another reason for the male preference of placing bets on short-term outcomes lies in the psychological and emotional experience gained from these types of gambling. This is in the 'buzz', the 'rush', the 'thrill' experienced through the activity.

However we may choose to scientifically explain the feelings attached to placing bets, the simple fact remains that the feelings gained from it are hugely exciting. When we feel such a high level of excitement it is like a shot in the arm of exhilaration coursing through our veins, and we experience a transcendent quality. We are lifted above day-to-day life, with all its mundane routine, and stresses and strains; we feel invincible. It is arguably, therefore, another form of escapism. It becomes addictive because of the extreme high that it gives. Highs can be great, and we all need a little sparkle in life, something to look forward to. If we can take it or leave it, no problem. By the stage gambling has become problematic, however, the high has become something that is consistently craved. By comparison, life outside gambling time appears uninteresting and lacking in stimulation. It seems no other thrill can match that of the ultimate thrill of the gambling activity. Here is a memorable comment from a 35-year-old professional man I had worked with, as he struggled to become free of his 15 years of problem gambling: 'Everything feels grey and dead, including me. At least when I was gambling I felt alive' (anonymous, four months into recovery).

Often, men who have developed problems with the aforementioned modes of gambling will describe the *anticipation* of a win as being the most enticing aspect of play. It is that period of uncertainty and hope that enables total concentration in the moment, in the gambling activity, through those intense feelings of anticipation. Keeping the excitement simmering. The win brings it to boiling point, but then already the simmering down begins. Placing another bet regains the desired anticipation.

As well as anecdotal evidence, research into male and female patterns of problem gambling behaviour has shown that one of the key differences in male and female problem gambling is in the modes of gambling they tend to favour. The reason for their choice is in the experiences provided by the type of gambling activity (Yale School of Medicine, 2012). We have looked, for example, at the experience of the male problem gambler who places bets and gets hooked into the high, craving more and more of that fix.

The different experiences to be gained from particular modes of gambling are comparable to those available from the use of certain recreational drugs (Nguyen, 2011). Forms of gambling that are equivalent to the rush experienced from taking cocaine, for example, are more likely to be favoured by men. Women tend to favour forms of gambling equivalent to the experience of smoking cannabis, such as slot machine playing or gambling online. I think this comparison also illustrates the narcotic effect of gambling, and that consciousness and emotional experience are altered in much the same way as by drugs or alcohol. So, withdrawal can be every bit as difficult.

In more recent years, another form of gambling that has often been reported by men for whom gambling has got out of control is the fixed odds betting terminal (FOBT). Being quickly caught in a cycle of loss chasing, anecdotally, has proved to be an issue. The FOBT allows players to bet on games and events with fixed odds. Games include roulette, which I hear reported as the most popular game, bingo, horse racing, dog racing and slot machine games.

Although, as we have seen, women who develop gambling problems often do so with slot machines, those who report gambling on FOBTs tend to be in the minority. However, I have noticed a slight increase in numbers over time. Women who have chosen to play FOBTs have often reported having done so because there were no amusement arcades in their vicinity, or they had a job that brought them into regular contact with FOBT machines, such as work in a betting shop. A main reason for few women playing FOBTs is that these machines are based in bookmakers' shops. We have already covered how that environment is not one in which many women feel comfortable, it still having a reputation for being one of the last bastions of masculinity. One woman who regularly attended group meetings was told by other group members when discussing her FOBT problem that she was 'brave' to enter the bookmaker's.

The larger stakes available when playing FOBTs (ranging from £1 to £500), and the rapidity of play also mean that, for someone for whom gambling is out of control, time spent in play can be minimal, thereby limiting the escape from reality that the female problem gambler is frequently seeking. Many women also report not being attracted to games that they perceive as involving a level of skill, or which they do not understand, because an element of the escapism is easy repetition of the chosen activity. If women do play FOBTs problematically, they report an initial 'buzz' from a win more frequently than women slot machine players do, but continued play then seems to settle them into a state of total absorption in much the same way as women who gamble on slot machines or online, but often with a faster downward spiral into debt because they are using more money to play and gain the desired experience.

The point at which male and female problem gamblers most often meet and have the most commonalities in terms of shared practical, psychological and emotional experience would be in the areas of both slot machine and online gambling. I have found that for the male gambler who is gambling excessively online, or on slot machines, just as for a woman engaging in the same behaviour, he is likely to be doing so for reasons of escapism, in a way that is not via a buzz but about the experience of total focus and absorption. Sometimes, I have known men speak of wanting to escape the thoughts and feelings associated with earlier catastrophic losses made by betting on horses, for example. They report gambling online to numb their feelings, as some might drink or take drugs for the same affect. Often, men who gamble excessively online have experienced at some point in life what a very high proportion of women problem gamblers have: that is, trauma. Or, at very least, they have good reason to find an aspect of day-to-day life something they desire to block out.

So, the reason for a gender difference in the chosen modes of gambling can be accounted for in part by location, the normalisation of the experience through its being modelled by same-gender parents, and the particular emotional and psychological reward that the individual is seeking from gambling.

If we examine the deeper psychological reasons for gambling becoming a woman's 'drug of choice', as opposed to substance misuse, for example, we find these reasons in the fact that gambling seems to her to provide what she craves, emotionally and psychologically. Gambling meets needs that she feels unable to have met in her life outside the comfort zone of excessive gambling:

I'm in a bubble . . . Nothing else can get inside. (Anonymous women's group member, 48 years old, gambling on slot machines)

They pull you in, those machines do. (Anonymous women's group member, 45 years old, gambling on slot machines)

It feels like hiding under the duvet – that kind of feeling that the world can't get at you. (Anonymous woman in one-to-one therapy, 42 years old, gambling online)

It's like another world, a fantasy world, it's hard to describe . . . but it's like I can't come back to this world again. (Lucy, women's group member, 33 years old, gambling online)

These quotes are from women describing their experience of gambling excessively on slot machines and online gambling sites. The sense of being 'pulled into' the machine or computer screen; completely drawn into a consciousness-altering experience of flashing lights and sound, into another world where nothing matters other than that moment; the repetition of pressing buttons or computer keys . . . That is a universal description of slot machine gambling, and online gambling.

It is that total focus on the activity that creates a hypnotic, trance-like effect. For that time, nothing else bothers the player, unaware of her surroundings or any others around her because she has paid to play herself into another world. No unwanted thoughts can penetrate the bubble she is in, and, as a result, no unpleasant feelings are aroused. She feels, at that time, and for as long as money for play lasts, that she is completely in control of her psychological and emotional experience. That I realise might sound an odd statement to make, because anyone who has known well a woman whose gambling is a problem will have seen her experience crashing lows on leaving her time in the arcade where she plays her slot machine, or on turning off her computer; will have seen and maybe heard her drowning in a sea of remorse, guilt and self-loathing; will have known that she is riddled with anxiety as to how she will survive until the next pay day having spent all available finances; will have witnessed her buying as much time out of her subjective reality as she possibly could. How on earth does this represent her feeling in control?

Such a women feels in control, despite this pain, because these are such familiar feelings. If she has been gambling for any significant length of time at all, she will have lived through these feelings time and time again, and for that very reason they have become predictable. No less painful than they were the first time she felt the true awfulness of what her excessive gambling had done to damage her finances, self-esteem and general quality of life, but at least she knows what it is she will feel. What she does not know is how to deal with the feeling that created the urge to gamble in the first place. The emotional or psychological trigger is experienced as *intolerable*. Gambling is an attempt to control whatever it is she feels is terrifyingly out of control within her emotional and psychological world, so much so that she never allows herself to identify with the feared experience. And so she swaps that unknown, out-of-control emotional and psychological world for the analgesic effect of the gambling world, and the predictable pain to follow: 'Better the devil you know . . .'

When speaking of gambling, I am sprinkling the page with similes speaking of the 'analgesic' qualities of gambling: the 'drug-like effect', the sense of women seeking a mellowing, relaxing, consciousness-altering sensation that might just as easily be gained by cannabis smoking, for example. Why, I am sure we might ask, does she choose gambling and *not* drugs or alcohol? On paper, I am sure it would make rational sense. Certainly, she would of course avoid the huge and often catastrophic financial consequences that are the cost of problem gambling. Many of the women who have come forward for treatment have indeed spent time in the world of drug or alcohol misuse. Those who have not have sometimes commented that they wish they had 'chosen' addiction to a substance because at least their financial situation would not have been devastated to the extent that it had been through gambling. In one extreme case, a woman shared that she wished she was still anorexic (her previous form of emotional management) because at least it would not have led her to bankruptcy, as her gambling had.

Gambling makes sense to the woman who develops the problem, despite the financial cost. In the moment she experiences the seemingly irresistible urge to gamble, it feels like a price worth paying – that she will risk gambling *at all costs*. She is buying her way out of her emotional pain and conflict, and buying time engaged in the activity of pure escapism.

Drugs and alcohol might be a cheaper alternative, but they come with their own price tag attached too. If we drink or we take drugs, they, like gambling, alter our consciousness, so in that sense they serve a similar purpose. A part of their effect, too, is that they send to sleep our inner censor – the part of us that weight up the appropriateness or healthiness of our behaviour and choices. That is one of the attractive things about the very experience of course – that it helps us to let go of inhibitions –

but if we take it too far, and put our inner sensor into a coma, we do not make good, healthy choices for ourselves and can therefore leave ourselves vulnerable.

Drugs and alcohol have an immediate physiological impact on the user far greater than that of gambling on the problem gambler. Eventually, problem gambling certainly does make a physical impact: stress and anxiety, and the resulting adrenalin sent coursing around the body, does take its toll. But the effects do not as often, or as intensely, leave the gambler feeling completely out of control of her body, as alcohol or drug misuse might.

The feeling of being able to alter consciousness but in a perceived controlled way is, in my professional experience, a very important factor in a woman's choice – be it conscious or unconscious – of problem gambling over drugs or alcohol.

As we have already seen, a very high percentage of women who have presented for problem gambling treatment are single parents. The demands of the job of single parenthood are pretty much relentless if so much as a 'good enough' job is to be done. Running the home, balancing the finances, trying to make ends meet, trying to fill the vacancy left by the absent parent all create intense pressures and anxieties and leave very little time and financial resources for activities outside the home and role of mother that might create some breathing space.

For the woman who finds herself lonely, anxious, depressed and unsupported, practically and emotionally, it can be tempting to turn more frequently to whatever it is she discovers eases her burden for a while. Alcohol and drugs might do the trick, but will in all likelihood impede her ability to turn up at the school gates on time, or to get up in time for work: to generally keep up the delicately balanced house of cards that is her life. What she discovers is that at first gambling does not affect her ability to function. She can buy her carefully allocated 'time out', and when she leaves the gambling bubble there are no obvious signs of her having an addiction problem as there would be with other forms of substance misuse. She can go back into her life, and pick up her responsibilities with no hangover to cope with, no spaced-out drug trip to hinder her carefully structured routine. At first she often feels that her gambling actually *helps* her to function, to take her responsibilities seriously and to do the best job she can.

Gambling for the single woman who is bringing up her family alone is often an attempt to do her best that has gone horribly wrong. The consequences, of course, can be that the children then suffer: they can be neglected as she gets pulled further and further into the world of gambling, craving more and more time with the experience. What I have learnt is that that has not been the intention. The *intention* is almost always to find a way to cope with fulfilling her overwhelming responsibilities. As one woman said to her group:

> I can see that as much as I hate it now my gambling helped me to survive. I didn't have anyone else, just me and the kids, and it was the only thing I had for me. I know it sounds weird, but in an odd kind of way, at the time gambling saved me, or I might not be here now.

Of course, not all women who have gambling problems are isolated and alone with children. Some women are holding down demanding careers where, again, a presence of mind is as essential to the job as it is for the woman bringing up children alone. The following quote I think illustrates the very conscious choice to gamble to switch off from the pressures and strains of the working day, which had left the woman not enough time, and too exhausted, to keep up with friends and family who might have helped to ease her mind:

> I used to take a lot of recreational drugs for a few years, but it was starting to affect my performance at work. Then I discovered that if I gambled online I could get the same kind of relaxed feelings, but still be fine at work the next day. (Christine, 39 years old)

Again, we can see how the escapism of gambling gives the sense of being in control. Being in control of thoughts and feelings that are unwanted by blocking them out, and – very importantly, and something that sets gambling apart from drug and alcohol abuse – in a way that gives a woman a sense of *being in control of her physical self*. She is able to walk away without the unwelcome residual affects of substance misuse. Until the behaviour becomes problematic, she will still able to function in her life.

The ability to remain in control, or at least to have a feeling of being in control, however illusory it may transpire to be, feels especially vital to the 84 per cent of women who have attended women's groups and are survivors of abuse or domestic violence. Their experiences in damaging relationships have left them with evidence that bad things happen if they are not in control. At the hands of others who have assumed power and control over them, they have received treatment of the very worst kind that wounded them perhaps physically, but, in whatever form their abuse came, it is the damage on a psychological and emotional level that has left the deepest scar.

One result of this wounding is a deeply rooted lack of trust in relationship. If we do not have close others, or feel we cannot allow ourselves to trust others to be close, to support us and help us *express* what bothers us, we often attempt to *suppress* our troubling feelings. Gambling as a means of emotional suppression is attractive to the woman who has experienced abuse or domestic violence because it feels essential to her to maintain control of her physiological self while attempting to gain control over her thoughts and emotions through her addictive behaviour. Gambling alters her consciousness enough for her to forget what is troubling her, but leaves her conscious enough not to feel physically vulnerable.

Not for her the out-of-control and unpredictable physical sensations that accompany many other forms of addiction. The repetition of slot machine play or gambling online, focusing on the computer screen, is reassuringly familiar and, importantly, predictable. Any feelings associated with that activity are equally so. Not for her, either, the forms of gambling such as horse racing or the casino table that might give a thrill of anticipation. She is not playing to feel *something*, but ultimately to feel *nothing*. She does not crave the feeling of anticipation like the male gambler who gets a thrill from betting, or placing stakes in the casino. Anticipation is uncertainty, and she diligently avoids uncertainty because her experience been that there are rarely nice surprises and often nasty ones. It feels essential for her to have that sense of predictability, that sense of being in control.

What I am not wanting to imply is that gambling to excess is the panacea for all women's problems: putting a woman back in the driving seat of her life by putting her in control of her thoughts and feelings, so that life is okay as a result. Of course, ultimately the process reverses, and sends her skidding completely off the road, more out of control than ever before. However, in order to be clear how she falls from a position of social or regular gambling into the trap of problem gambling, we need to understand how the choice of gambling makes sense to her.

Experience has shown me that it is this conscious or unconscious wish to avoid dependency on anything, or anyone, that might leave a woman feeling physically out of control and vulnerable, which is a huge factor in her becoming a problem gambler, as opposed to a problem drinker or drug user. Indeed it may have influenced her cross-addiction from substances to problem gambling.

It is interesting to note that 50 per cent of women whom I have treated in a women's group have also had (or still have, at the time of presenting for treatment) a history of self-harm (for example, cutting or burning) or eating disorders.

During treatment we have identified these behaviours too, as coping mechanisms, with traits similar to problem gambling. These behaviours have also been ways of attempting to manage perceived intolerable thoughts and feelings and, as with gambling, doing so in a way in which a woman has a sense of gaining emotional control through focus on a behaviour, without the feared loss of physical control, consciousness and associated vulnerability that is the likely result of drug or alcohol misuse.

Another thread that connects problem gambling, self-harm and eating disorders is the element of secrecy that is possible with all these methods of emotional management. If we believe, however erroneously, that something we do is helping us to cope, or even is essential to our very survival, does it not make sense that we want to hold on to it tightly? If we can keep our coping mechanism hidden, we increase the chances of keeping a hold on it.

Because the physiological symptoms are less obvious than with substance abuse, problem gambling is so much more easily hidden than drug or alcohol misuse. If our 'drug of choice' remains hidden, we also avoid the judgement of others, the shame attached to being perceived as unable to cope, to being an 'addict', and of course the shame of being caught in the act of being less than what we expect of ourselves. We may avoid the ultimate pain of beginning to look at ourselves.

So, we are beginning to see how, despite the obvious associations gambling has with *risk*, far from making a choice to gamble with the intention of taking a risk, or being reckless, the woman who gambles problematically is using the activity of gambling to attempt to be, or at least to *feel*, in control of her life, or some aspect of her life or inner self that troubles her relentlessly, and which feels to her beyond her power and resources to control.

The part of any of us that develops addictive behaviour *feels* as though it has no choice other than to be swept along with the cravings for whatever it may be that gives us our fix. That part of us feels *as if* it has no choice, despite the fact that it may make no rational sense at all to others around us or even to ourselves when we are in our moments of greater clarity, when we have respite from the situational, psychological and emotional triggers that create the urge and subsequent behaviour. In those moments when we are in our *adult* selves, we can reflect on the irrationality and destructiveness of our addictive behaviour and despairing with ourselves ask, 'What was I thinking of?' That is the thing. We were not thinking, we were reacting to intense feelings and emotions, and craving what we felt we needed in that moment, regardless of the logical consequences. In those moments, we were *childlike*.

Another reason for the choice of gambling over other forms of escapism and emotional management lies in that for some women gambling has a positive resonance with feeling childlike. For a woman pulled into gambling by this hook, gambling leads back to happier times in childhood when she felt more secure and safe, and there were adults to shield her from the burdens of life she now struggles with. Seaside holidays, visiting amusement arcades, pushing pennies into the slot machine were innocent fun. In times in later life, when crisis hits, she finds herself drawn to pick up the thread that leads back to activities that have an association with those good feelings.

One woman identified her most lucid memory of happiness as the annual family visit to the funfair. She described in detail how she would relish being wrapped up in the sensational experience of the bright lights and sounds and smells. In later life, she suffered a series of experiences in relationship and work life that left her afraid to venture too far from her home, and eventually this meant the loss of her career. She became increasingly isolated and depressed, and fell into an escalating pattern of slot machine gambling in arcades. We identified that, when she felt the urge to gamble in an amusement arcade, unconsciously, the sad, scared little girl within her was running down the garden path and back to the fun fair. The lights and sounds in the arcade were reminiscent of that time when she had felt so happy and safe.

For women who gamble online, the soft fuzzy colours or bright primaries can be reminiscent of playing computer games as a child or disappearing into the wonderful world of the Disney film where, in even the most tragically painful of situations, everything always turns out all right in the end.

I have heard the experience described as being as if the world of online gambling can flow into the real world for a time. Many hours spent staring at the screen mean that, even on pulling away, or being thrown out of that world because all money has been spent, the screen images are projected on the walls and carpet in front of the eyes, like a soft visual buffer, taking the rough edges off any harsh realities.

As we have identified, for the woman who develops a problem, the choice to gamble, conscious or unconscious, begins as an attempt to be in control, and to manage difficult emotional, psychological and general day-to-day life problems better, with the initial intention of dipping in and out of the behaviour as needed.

Profile of a recreational gambler

- Gambling is fun.
- There is a sense of 'I can take it or leave it'.
- Gambles only with affordable money.
- Gambles within time affordable recreational time.
- Gambles socially, or will openly discuss their gambling.

Profile of a problem gambler

- Gambling often no longer feels fun.
- The sense of 'take it or leave it' has gone, replaced by cravings.
- Gambling all available finances.
- Gambles at high cost to time spent in key relationships or other important activities.
- Gambling is often hidden and a woman with the problem is withdrawn, secretive and preoccupied.
- May experience erratic moods, and feel increasingly anxious and depressed.

So, at some point, for a woman who gambles problematically, the scales tip. The balance shifts from gambling as fun, as healthy escapism or measured emotional management, and her inner and outer worlds slip into chaos – exactly what she was fearing the most, and trying to avoid by gambling.

Chapter 3

Sliding into trouble

I am hopeful that by this stage I will have communicated that, through my practice, I have learnt that it is not the existence and availability of gambling that causes problems for women. Women who develop gambling problems have what they experience to be unresolvable problems in their external or internal world. The level of engagement to be had with gambling is on a spectrum, which I will now describe.

Social gambling

If we are social gamblers, we enjoy gambling as entertainment, as and when the occasion arises. We might have the odd day at the races, an evening at the casino, play a few slot machines in the arcade on a seaside trip; perhaps buy a lottery ticket if there is a rollover and we fancy our chances that week.

Regular gambling

Gambling is a regular part of our routine and established as a source of entertainment during our leisure time. Perhaps we budget for those weekly evenings at the bingo hall, or keep money in an account with our favourite online gambling sites. We find gambling enjoyable, and keep it within our financial means; as we might with membership at the gym.

Problem gambling

Our pattern of gambling is starting to cause us a few problems. Maybe we notice we are starting to spend a little too much time and money on the activity. Maybe we have not noticed it ourselves, but others close to us have commented that they question how healthy our pattern of gambling is. Gambling is starting to feel less about something we choose to do because it is a pleasure, but because we feel we *need* to gamble. We may be starting to use it as emotional management – like feeling the need for a cigarette or an extra glass of wine, after a hard day. It may not be problematic all day every day, but we possibly notice that there are times when we 'binge' and immerse ourselves in the activity, and emerge feeling the worse for it: financially, emotionally and psychologically.

Pathological gambling

Gambling is no longer just a part of our lives, but has permeated and is affecting all aspects of our lives. When not engaged in the gambling activity, we are completely preoccupied with it: either filled with guilt and anxiety over time and money wasted, or struggling with urges to gamble again. Finances, relationships, important areas of commitment such as work are suffering. All sense of fun has left the gambling activity, yet despite this we feel an irresistible pull to repeat the destructive cycle.

So why is it that the majority of women will remain at the start of the spectrum, as social or regular gamblers? Or, if they do begin to slide into problematic gambling, they can slide back to social or regular gambling again? I would suggest that the key is hidden – as with so many things in our lives – in our relationships.

Any form of addiction is essentially an attempt to cope with life and to remain living: to tolerate life. We often hear talk of the 'self-destructive' addict. Yes, the consequences of addiction are destructive. I have never met a woman, however, who wanted, consciously or unconsciously, to destroy herself with her gambling; on the contrary, women who gamble problematically tend to be *survivors*.

When exploring the reasons for any addiction, the phrase 'there but for the grace of God go I' might be appropriate for us to bear in mind. If we are fortunate, one way in which we survive the ups and downs of life is to talk things through with others in whom we trust:

> The talking that women do with friends is aimed at building intimacy. Indeed the most valued function of friendship for women of all ages appears to be intimacy-assistance: discussing private, personal feelings and receiving help . . . the encouragement, support and affirmation that women receive from female friends is linked to women of all ages and from diverse groups to positive feelings of well-being, high self-esteem, and life satisfaction. (Lips, 2006)

We have spent time in the first two chapters exploring the benefits of this, and how we are increasingly lacking in avenues to get this basic human need met in modern Western society.

A close friend of mine recently shared in a light-hearted but meaningful way her concern as to how much time she was spending playing her favourite sudoku game on her smartphone. My friend is enviably organised, conventional and completely all-round reliable, and yet she found herself so taken by the game that on a few occasions she lost track of time and was late for work. This had never happened previously.

On the surface, my friend lives an ordered and ordinary life with husband and children. However, a difficult few months with simultaneous family crises and taking care of, and worrying about, everyone in the family but herself, had had an impact. My friend tends to find it uncomfortable to share her feelings, and the situation had left her spiralling into stress and anxiety. Over a few cups of tea with friends, she recognised for herself what the reason was for her excessive gaming: she had found that concentrating on the game helped her to stop her anxiety-provoking thoughts for a time, and to find some respite. As a result, she was sliding down the scale to a level at which the game was becoming a problem. It was the talking things through and having space for reflection with others that helped to keep her problems, and therefore her playing, in perspective. It helped her to slide back to a more regular, less potentially harmful and more enjoyable scale of play.

My friend was beginning to experience the price we pay for investing more time than is affordable in even our seemingly very innocent forms of escapism. She was becoming preoccupied with what helped her to feel better – her gaming – and her life was just beginning to become a little messier as a result. She was beginning to find day-to-day commitments slipping. This in turn troubled her, added to her problems and made her want to play the game more and more.

Money of course was not involved in the playing of the sudoku game but, had it been, my friend might as well have been gambling. If you have read the previous chapters, you will now recognise that the absorption and escapism aspects of the game are so similar to those found in concentration on gambling. For the woman who gambles, but is financially well-off, it may take a considerable amount of time for her financial 'rock bottom' to be reached, but the unaffordable amount of time spent may cost her dear in damage to relationships and impact on other commitments.

The financial losses, which can be a heavy and more recognisable cost of gambling, can also speed up the slide along the spectrum from gambling being a bit of social fun, or regular escapism. This is an aspect particular to gambling, which makes it distinctive from other forms of addiction. Substantial sums of money might be spent by the class A drug user, but gambling stands alone in that it offers a realistic *hope*, however small it may be, however remote the odds may be, that money lost to addiction might be clawed back. One more bet, one more play could produce a win significant enough to lessen the pain of loss. Hanging on tightly to that hope, and to the distraction of the gambling activity in order to escape the worsened reality the behaviour caused, she spirals downward into a cycle of loss chasing. There seems no other option other than to continue to gamble.

What we are seeing is that over-investment of money *and* time are two primary factors for gambling moving from social or regular to problematic or pathological. Underpinning this over-investment, of course, may be distressing thoughts and feelings regarding past or current life situations, which drive a need for escapism.

As I have mentioned, I am fortunate to have learnt the majority of what I know about the area of women and problem gambling by listening to the life stories my clients have shared with me and by trying to help them to make sense of their gambling problem. In order to illustrate what has been discussed so far, I will now share elements of three women's stories.

Laura

On approaching therapeutic treatment, Laura was 36 years old and widowed, with no children. She was unemployed and on medication for depression. She had been gambling for three years on online bingo sites. She had previously attended Gamblers Anonymous meetings.

Laura grew up in a family where she was the youngest of five children. Her parents both had alcohol problems and as a consequence were often unemployed. The preoccupation of their addictions meant they did not have the capacity for money management and, as a result, Laura remembers often feeling humiliated at being sent to borrow money or food from neighbours or hiding behind the sofa when debt collectors called. She would often miss out on joining in with her peer group at school because there was not enough money for treats such as the school disco, and she was often embarrassed by her unfashionable hand-me-down clothes.

Laura was determined to avoid falling into the poverty trap she witnessed her parents in. She studied hard at school and aimed to attend college, but the problems at home meant that she found it hard to concentrate on her work. On leaving school with few exams, she took a succession of low-paid jobs in care homes for the elderly, which bored her. She worked long hours, however, and took on extra shifts despite hating her job. Having grown up with very little, she felt delighted at being able to at last buy herself some of the clothes and treats she had lacked as a child. Never having been taught sound financial management, or seen it modelled by her parents, she quickly found herself falling into debt.

Relationships were also a challenging area for Laura. She had few close friends and at work she struggled with her colleagues and remained distant and sensitive to perceived criticism, always feeling as if she were the outsider in the group. She also found relationships with men a problem, finding she quickly became attached and overly dependent to the point that the other person would feel overwhelmed and end the relationship.

At the age of 28, Laura met a much older man and married him. She imagined that here at last were the stability and security she had craved throughout her life. She found herself disappointed when her husband did not meet her expectations in terms of caring for her emotionally, but financially she was more at ease than she had ever been because he paid off her debts and took responsibility for the bills. Five years into their marriage, her husband suffered a fatal heart attack. She described this time as one in which she felt abandoned and unable to cope alone. She became deeply depressed, could not motivate herself to go to work and began once again to fall into debt.

One evening, while spending time on the internet, Laura discovered an online bingo site and, remembering having once enjoyed a game of bingo at a bingo hall with her sisters, she decided to play. She was pleased to quickly have a substantial win, which eased the pressure of that month's bills, and she found that she enjoyed the winning feelings, which lifted her depression for a time. She began to gamble on the bingo site regularly, finding that for the time she was playing she did not think about her fears of being alone in the world, or her increasing debt. It was a good feeling, too, to sometimes win some money when all her life had been such a financial struggle and money was so hard to earn and even harder to manage. For a time, she found gambling helpful to her emotional and psychological well-being.

After a few weeks, Laura began to realise she was gambling with more and more money that she could not afford. It was at this point that the inevitable financial losses were so painful to bear that she would find herself panic-stricken to the point of feeling physically sick. She described the first time she spent her rent money for the month in one day, feeling a level of shame that was beyond her verbal expression. She felt like a hysterical, panic-stricken child. All her instincts told her to keep playing; perhaps she might win it back. She had to hang on to that hope.

Laura's case illustrates how investing unaffordable amounts of money in gambling can escalate quickly into a downward spiral of loss chasing. It is important to note that, even though the focus for her was on winning back her money, through the course of therapy she became aware that what she was chasing was not only her money but also the *feelings* of being a winner again. The winning feelings for her were initially an antidepressant, and associated with feeling secure. For her, money represented security. Therefore, having no money left her feeling vulnerable – just as we are when we are children. It was her childlike memories and fears that hooked her in to loss chasing.

As Laura described, her early life was fraught with insecurities and feelings of embarrassment and shame, all associated with lack of money. This, as we see, had an impact on her later ability to relate. Her difficulty in 'joining in' at work, feeling that she was being talked about and not part of the group were all connected to her feeling ashamed of her poverty-stricken childhood, where her peers laughed at her shabby clothes. Her parents were unreliable and did not meet even her most basic needs or teach her valuable life skills such as money management and facing and resolving problems. When as an adult she became involved with a man, she would cling on for dear life, hoping that here at last was someone who would take care of her. When she began to lose money gambling, despite her being in the physical body of a 34-year-old woman, she felt childlike again. The rent money was gone and in its place were all the old feelings of shame, embarrassment and insecurity she had experienced in childhood. Overwhelmed by her strong feelings, she panicked – as children do – and could feel only the desperate need to win the money back. If she did so, she was certain she the feelings would stop.

When the hoped-for big win did not materialise and Laura's anxiety and depression grew, in a sense the world of online gambling replaced the sofa to hide behind from the debt collectors. If she focused on playing, she was not thinking; for that time, therefore, she was feeling nothing about her growing financial problems and could hide away from that painful reality.

Laura realised during therapy that her relationship with gambling had at first unconsciously provided her with a sense of the okay parent she had never had; it helped her to manage her feelings and – she fantasised – met her financial needs. For a time her husband had met those needs. During therapy she came to think that she had married him wanting him to be the parent she had never had. When he died, although rationally she knew he had not chosen to abandon her, she felt abandoned, and this compounded her beliefs that relationships were not to be trusted. It seemed no other individual could meet her needs and she felt unable to act autonomously as an adult in the world, because she had never been taught healthy life skills by her parents and she had been sheltered from developing in these areas by her husband.

Ultimately, of course, Laura's relationship with gambling mirrored that of the reality of her upbringing and the lack of money, sense of shame and insecurities she suffered. It was at the point at which she started to re-experience these overwhelming feelings that she slid rapidly down the scale from social to pathological gambling.

Emily

When she came into our women's group, Emily was 41. She was divorced and a single parent to two children in their late teens. She was unemployed because of chronic ill health. She had been gambling for 20 years on slot machines and had attended one-to-one therapy.

Emily was the youngest of three sisters and was born into a family where addiction was a problem for her father. He was a regular drug user and would at times beat her mother, which Emily sometimes witnessed. Since she was a baby, Emily had been regularly looked after by friends of the family, at times when her mother could not cope. By the time she reached the age of 16, she had left her dysfunctional family home. Shortly after this, she met and quickly married a man who was soon to become the father of her two sons.

It soon became apparent to Emily that her husband had a drug problem. Like her father, he was often absent from home and she was left to cope alone with the children. The couple separated and the husband's addiction meant that he rarely paid child maintenance, or helped with childcare. Emily was determined that her children would not experience the same kind of neglect and abandonment that she herself had experienced as a child, and she set out to be the opposite kind of mother to the one she had known herself. Severe physical health problems meant that she was unable to work, and she refused to leave her children with babysitters to take time for herself.

By the time her sons began to attend school, Emily's isolated lifestyle had left her with no friends, and her only adult contact was through her still difficult relationship with her parents.

One day, after the school run, Emily wandered into an amusement arcade and found herself playing a slot machine. She enjoyed the feeling of winning a little money, and found the lights and sounds attractive and a welcome distraction from her loneliness and boredom. She found herself playing regularly after that. She began to feel the arcade owners were friends, because they would ask about her day and her children. So began a pattern of gambling for Emily, which seemed to meet her needs for company and entertainment. She would spend almost every day while her children were at school in front of a fruit machine in the arcade. She found also that at times when she was sad or angry about her situation as a single parent, or indeed with her own parents, gambling would seem to help her to forget about that.

Ever careful with her money, throughout her 20 years of gambling five days each week, Emily never fell into debt, never neglected her children's needs in any area, never failed to meet any commitment. Her gambling was limited to regular hours, in the same arcade each time. What she did fail to do was develop a life for herself outside the family home, outside the amusement arcade. As her sons grew older, she began to realise that she had no identity other than that of mother, and no friends apart from the owners of the arcade. What prompted her to enter treatment was acknowledging to herself that she was now filled with fear at the thought of moving outside her comfort zone of home and amusement arcade.

Emily's story shows us that it is important not to focus exclusively on the amount of money that is lost to problem gambling, but the amount of time too. We can see how Emily's intention was to create the family that she had sadly lacked in her own childhood. Perhaps, unconsciously, she had chosen a man similar to her father, because it was a familiar relational dynamic. Most important for the purpose of understanding her gambling is that, during therapy, Emily discovered that her decision to marry an unpredictable and unreliable man then triggered her childhood feelings around abandonment and uncertainty. These feelings when evoked were so fresh, and provoked such intense fear within her, that she would go to any lengths to protect her children from experiencing anything remotely similar.

Emily set about to create a world for her children and herself where everything was predictable and therefore – she felt – as safe and secure as possible. She spoke in the group of her love of Disney films, which portrayed strong family values. She particularly loved the ending of films in which, no matter what crisis had beset the family, they would be all safe and happy, together under the same roof.

To Emily, a part of her keeping her family safe meant maintaining a sealed family unit where nobody unfamiliar gained entry. By this stage she did not trust her own judgement, having married a man like her father, who had betrayed her trust. We can see perhaps how the 'safe house' Emily built began to feel a little like a prison, and how tempting it might have been to be seduced by the new experience of playing a slot machine. It offered a little stimulation, but in a safe and predictable way.

'Friends' in the arcade were people Emily could talk to, safe from the perceived dangers of emotional intimacy. Her childhood and marriage had given her evidence that, if she got close to someone, they let her down. A conversation with someone in the arcade about the latest television programme or day-to-day issues took the edge off of her aching loneliness, but in a way that avoided true intimacy developing.

For Emily, predictability was vital. Uncertainty brought up all her intolerable childhood feelings connected with abandonment. It was an easy next step then for her gambling to become a part of her day-to-day routine, so essential to her feeling safe. It became an extension of her world over which she felt in control because she could play at regular times, in the same arcade, surrounded by familiar faces. She began to slide into problem gambling when she began to associate gambling with changing her emotional experience. Feeling sad was deeply distressing to her. When we feel sad, we feel vulnerable. For Emily, life had presented her with few opportunities for feeling safe enough to feel vulnerable; as a consequence, she allowed nobody close enough to talk through her feelings and so, in a sense, the slot machine represented that okay parent or best friend – helping her with her feelings, but by suppression, rather than the expression offered by healthy, intimate relationship.

Ruth

Ruth was 48 years old, divorced and had a son and daughter in their early twenties. Her son, who was disabled, still lived at home. She had just returned to work, having been unemployed for five years after suffering a breakdown. She had gambled for 15 years on slot machines in arcades. She attended one-to-one therapy and women's group meetings.

Ruth grew up as the youngest of three children. She never knew her father and was brought up by her mother. For reasons she never learnt, her elder brother and sister were sent to live with other members of her extended family when she was 3 years old. She and her mother lived a nomadic lifestyle: moving home often to avoid her mother's debt problems. Her mother began to leave her at home alone, often for the whole night. Ruth described feeling terrified of being alone in the dark and the only way she could experience a degree of comfort would be to switch on every light in the flat in which they lived.

When her mother returned from her nights away, Ruth's terrors were far from over. She was never sure 'which mother was coming home'. At best, her mother would be silent and cold towards her; at worst, she would be physically abusive and cruel to her. Ruth began to keep as silent and as still as she could in her mother's presence. She did not understand what she could have done wrong to make her mother so angry with her, and so she thought that if she was as still and quiet as possible it would lessen the chance of enraging her.

Ruth continued to suffer physical and psychological abuse and neglect from her mother all through her childhood. She did not disclose the abuse because her mother had told her things would get worse if she were to tell, and that, even if she did tell, nobody would believe her. At the age of 16, Ruth left home and went to college, and she described that period as the best time of her life. She enjoyed her studies and valued her independence, and she felt she could finally begin to be herself. At 18, she met and married an older man who seemed to offer her the stability, love and protection she craved. She went on to take a responsible job in social care.

After their first child was born, Ruth began to experience flashbacks from the abuse she suffered as a child. She felt as if there were no escape. She began to self-harm, finding that cutting herself offered temporary escape from her feelings. On wandering into an arcade in her lunch break, she discovered that playing a slot machine had a similarly calming affect. She was struck by how immediately drawn into the machines she was, and described her gambling as becoming instantly problematic. There was something about the environment and the lights and sounds from the slot machines that she found strangely comforting and soothing.

Ruth shows us how the path to problem or pathological gambling does not have to be one along which we proceed neatly from the social end of the scale and progress to problem or pathological gambling. It is possible to enter straight at the problem or pathological end of the spectrum. For some people, as for Ruth, there is something that is instantly bewitching. After a couple of months of one-to-one therapy, we identified that for Ruth slot machine arcades unconsciously offered her that same self-soothing mechanism that she had developed as a child. By surrounding herself with the lights from the slot machines in the arcade, she was 'putting all the lights on' in the flat, when she felt the same level of fear as she had when she was that 3-year-old child.

For Ruth, playing a slot machine met all her criteria for strategies on how to survive that she had developed in childhood. As children, even though we may not be consciously aware of it, we make decisions as to how survive in life based on how to please our parents, or caregivers. After all, if we have a hope of surviving, we are going to need them around because we cannot feed, clothe, protect ourselves. Ruth, as we have heard from her story, worked out that to remain as still and as quiet as possible was her greatest chance of survival, in terms of having a chance of not only getting her needs met, but also of avoiding attack.

Ruth carried these rules for survival into adulthood and into her marriage. When her first child was born, memories of her own childhood triggered flashbacks. Unconsciously, she quickly unpacked her old survival skills. Both gambling and self-harm helped her to stay quiet, and not to 'tell' about her increasingly distressing feelings about her past. Both behaviours were distractions from her inner pain. If she played a slot machine often enough, for long enough, she could avoid hearing her own inner voice, which told of how afraid and miserable she felt. If she could suppress her feelings in that way, there was less urge to break that 'Don't tell' rule, and risk telling another about the abuse she had suffered. She was still utterly convinced by what her mother had told her, that nobody would believe her, and that something bad would happen if she dared to tell. Keeping herself shut off from others who might have supported her in making positive changes, it seemed to her as though her only option was to avoid her own thoughts and feelings, as often as she could, through the comfort and escape of gambling.

Laura, Emily and Ruth all entered the spectrum of gambling at different points. Despite this, at assessment, all three would meet the criteria in the *DSM* screen for problem or pathological gambling. We might understand how it was their lack of healthy relationships, and/or lack of confidence and trust to engage openly with another that made it so much easier for the gambling problem to continue and worsen. In each case, their gambling was easily hidden. In the cases of Laura and Emily, there were no adults present in their lives to notice, be concerned by or comment on perceived changes in mood or behaviour. For all three, given their childhood and adult life experiences, how much safer it might have felt to avoid taking the risk of getting close enough to another to confide the gambling problems, or the underlying problems that had led to the slide into problem gambling.

Chapter 4

Escaping to a trap

In Chapter 3, we saw how three women slid down the spectrum of gambling behaviour to become problem or pathological gamblers, because gambling at first seemed to them to be a satisfying, soothing substitute for the healthy relationships that were sadly lacking in their lives, and that they were afraid to invite in. If an individual is using gambling to meet needs, and from their frame of reference make improvements in psychological and emotional states, should it then be termed 'problematic? Maybe, maybe not. Perhaps if for a moment we put aside all the various screens for diagnosis of problem gambling, what truly defines it as a problem is whether or not the activity is affecting, in an adverse way, the life of the woman who gambles and/or those close to her.

Arguably, many of us have ways of coping with life now and then that on personal reflection, or on receiving the judgement of others, may not be the healthiest way of getting by. If they do not cause problems for us or for others, or put blocks on our life path that stop us being where we would wish to be, maybe they are not problematic forms of behaviour, even though in terms of values or morals they may not be judged as healthy. What we began to see was that for Laura, Emily and Ruth, however, life outside the world of gambling felt so harsh, unmanageable and lonely that they began investing more and more time and money in their escapism. They felt as if they could depend on it to help them through life. Despite their perception being that gambling was of benefit to their psychological and emotional well-being, it became detrimental, a problem and unhealthy.

We have already identified that overspending of time and money leads only to an intensifying of the original problems that led to gambling, which perpetuates the destructive cycle. Ruth's story illustrates that for a few women gambling is problematic from the start. For the majority of women, however, not only is there a point at which their gambling slides from being recreational, or regular, to problematic, or pathological, but also a point at which there is a switch in the role gambling plays in a woman's life, from her perceived 'rescuer' to her 'persecutor'.

Through what we have covered so far, we know that one of the obvious yet important factors that causes gambling to become an additional problem is the amount of money that can be spent and lost, leading to losses then being chased. We often hear talk about 'the gambler' and gamblers' complete lack of respect for money or sense of its value. It tends not to be that a woman gambles excessively because she sees no value in money, but more that her excessive gambling leads to a change in her perception of money. Money becomes just a means of buying herself whatever she feels she needs from gambling at that time. Women, as we are aware, tend to choose modes of gambling that create a sense of unreality and switch off conscious thought processes. And because of just that sense of detachment, no attention is paid to the amount of money spent. Gambling online lends itself very well to the sense of fantasy, and detachment from the value of money, because there is no cash – the transaction is out in the ether. One woman described her spending money playing online as just pressing numbers: she had no sense at that time of those numbers representing a drain on her bank account, until the bubble around that moment in time burst.

Conversely, I have seen women who would beg, steal or borrow money to gamble when caught in the eye of their gambling storm, become very aware of every penny spent when established in recovery. One lighter moment in the group was when one member commented on how expensive coffee was at the café, opposite our meeting. Then she reflected, and laughed at how ludicrous she thought it sounded to resent spending £2.50 when £250 put into a fruit machine would have felt nothing at the time of a craving. What had she felt she was buying herself that was worth such a high cost? Whatever it was, it was likely to have seemed to her that only gambling could provide it.

Some women, even when in the worst periods of their gambling problem, still manage to budget for the essentials in life, the rational parts of their brains knowing that they will need money for the children's lunch, or the bus home from the arcade. They keep some money aside from 'gambling money' in a separate purse or pocket, or leave money at home, or a credit card with a friend. They know that when the craving for gambling arises they cannot trust themselves with money; that, even though they understand the consequences, the part of them that is desperate to gamble cannot be trusted to remain aware, or indeed at that moment care about consequences, so that all money will then become 'gambling money'.

'Just in case . . .' It was described simply, and effectively as that, by two women in the group who were discussing why they each had remained trapped in uncontrolled gambling. They spoke of how they continued to feed more money into the slot machine, to buy one more scratchcard, because the next one could be the win they were by that stage financially desperate for. And who knows? It always might be so. That is, after all, the gamble.

The thing is that any woman who has spent any time at all in the tangled mess that problem gambling creates is well aware on some level that she is fooling herself, if she believes that a significant win might buy her way out of the prison that her gambling behaviour has become. The win might solve some of the financial problems caused by excessive gambling, and ease any urges to loss chase. If the underlying problems that triggered the gambling still exist, however, why would it feel like it makes sense to stop gambling, after the win? In fact, some women speak of the relief of having lost all their money:

> At least then, I could go home. I had to stop. I was exhausted, I hadn't eaten or been to the toilet in hours. I'd had enough, but I knew if I won any more, I'd have kept gambling. I can never walk away with money.

> It makes me sick to think about it. I won £500, and then put it all back. It's mad, but I was hoping I wouldn't win any more, because I knew I'd be stuck there, staring at the computer screen. I just wanted to get rid of it.

> I stayed there all day. All day. When I got home, I had blisters on my fingers from pressing the buttons. I hate it, but I kept winning, telling myself I'd leave in five minutes and who am I kidding?

I have witnessed women, physically tense, shaking, literally pulling at their hair, their faces screwed up with the tension and anxiety they are describing as they speak of the act of repetitive gambling. Their body language speaks what often no words can of their painful and distressing experience.

As I wrote the word 'painful', I found myself thinking how that word could summarise so much of what drives continued problem gambling on a psychological and emotional level. The experience of a woman telling herself the truth – that her coping mechanism has failed – the pain involved in acknowledging, let alone accepting that, in what is often already a life brimful of emotional difficulty, can feel just too painful to bear. Gambling lifted her deflated spirits, made her feel good and helped her to hide from her problems. As the financial losses come thick and fast, as she tries to win back what she has lost and loses more, she feels her self-esteem, often already fragile, shatter. She also feels emotionally and psychologically beaten by the endlessly exhausting process. She doubts her strength and resources to break the destructive cycle.

Let us now hear the stories of two more women who will show us how their gambling became problematic.

Claire

Claire is 45 years old and has two adult children. At the time of her gambling problem, she was unemployed and a single parent, with her children in late teens. She had gambled for ten years on slot machines in arcades.

Claire had a history of eating disorder and diagnosed depression and anxiety. She had received counselling on previous occasions to address these issues, but had ended the process early both times because she found the counsellors too quick to touch on her family history, which included her troubled childhood as the child of a mother with mental health issues. She felt deep shame around these issues. Her daughter was diagnosed with autism, and she had found herself comfort eating at times of stress, to the point that she would be physically sick. Her weight gain as a result of her binge eating had been considerable, and she was diagnosed as clinically obese. When she came to therapy, her gambling was, to her, completely beyond her control. She was regularly playing slot machines with any available money and deeply in debt.

Gambling had been attractive to Claire because she had discovered early on that playing a slot machine gave her similar feelings of comfort to those gained from eating the sugar-laden foods she had craved to ease her depression and anxiety. Moreover, at first, gambling came with the bonus of being guilt free. There was no weight gain, no criticism of her appearance, from herself or others, and she could leave the arcade feeling okay to continue with the endless round of caregiving for her children and mother that was her life. More and more often when gambling, she would lose track of time and lose more money than she could afford. On a very tight budget, this would make her feel anxious and she began to chase her losses. When the hoped-for big win never came, or when she did have a win, she would put the money straight back into the machine. She began to borrow money from friends and family and soon fell into debt. She tried attending Gamblers Anonymous meetings but found the mainly male group dismissive of her fruit machine playing, and she feared their judgement if she attended meetings having gambled. Anxious to please and to fit in, she would have short gambling-free periods through sheer willpower alone, but found that at these times she would quickly slip back into her pattern of binge eating, which she detested herself for.

By this stage, Claire's daughter had become physically abusive to her, and her mother's always fragile mental health began to deteriorate. Claire found that the more sad and anxious and depressed she felt about her family life, the more she craved the soothing affects of playing a slot machine; afterwards, she would be full of self-loathing and the guilt present in her binge eating, which she had at first avoided feeling while gambling, began to creep in. This was compounded by the fact that she was beginning to be increasingly absent for her daughter. The worse Claire felt about her life, herself and her out-of-control gambling, the more she felt the overwhelming urge to gamble.

It is easy to see from Claire's story how the gambling self-soothing mechanism and then the process 'turned on her', as she would later describe it during therapy. Just like her mother often turned on her with her dramatic mood swings, which were the result of her condition. As a child, Claire had in effect never really had a mother. She had the physical presence of her mother, but her mother's mental heath problems meant that often her behaviour was embarrassing for Claire. Claire learnt how to self-soothe early on through sheer necessity. She told me how her kindly neighbour would bake her cakes, and she discovered that cakes and chocolate helped her to feel comforted and relaxed. It was at this point that the association between sweet food and comfort developed – the comfort that her mother was sadly unable to provide.

The shame that Claire felt as a child wounded her deeply and she would go to any lengths to avoid the feeling. She tells us in her story that once seen in what she perceived as a negative way by her doctor when labelled as obese, she was devastated. When she came across fruit machine playing, it initially seemed that here was her salvation. She had discovered a way of easing her psychological and emotional distress, but in a secretive way – no shame involved, no guilt involved because it was invisible, unlike the effects of her comfort eating.

Claire described her pattern of cross addiction from gambling to once again binge-eating in terms of absolute frustration and shame. At that early stage of therapy, she just could not comprehend her own behaviour: 'I am just stupid and greedy.' The comfort eating behaviour was so entrenched and had been going on for so long that it was an automatic process that she did not understand the meaning of herself. As a result, she focused only on the existence of the behaviour. The fact that she continued with behaviour that she knew was destructive filled her with anger and disappointment towards herself and she repeated the messages that she had received continually from her peers at school: that she was stupid, greedy and fat.

An additional message Claire now repeated to herself was the content of a note left one evening by her friend, while Claire was in the arcade, miserable and gambling. The note spoke of how her daughter was okay, but had called her mother's friend to get her tea and put her to bed again. It also said she knew it was because Claire was in the arcade, gambling. Claire collapsed into floods of tears when she read that note out loud to me during a therapy session. So great was her anger towards herself, she wanted to prove to me what a bad mother she was. She was absolutely convinced that, if only I truly knew her, I would stop caring for her and be full of criticism of her. After all, if she could not value anything about herself, how could I? How could anyone? It was a deeply moving moment to witness.

When Claire had originally received that note, would that not have been enough to make her stop gambling, when clearly she loved her daughter? Sadly, at that point even louder than the message of abandonment, and the unconditional love from her friend, were the messages of self-criticism and shame that Claire had internalised all through her life. To her, the note was clear evidence that she was no better a mother to her children than her own mother had been to her. The guilt and shame felt too excruciating to tolerate and, feeling too that she was not worthy of deserving help and support, she continued to seek the temporary soothing effect of gambling.

Gwen

Gwen was 50 years old, divorced and living with her second husband. She had no children from either relationship, but her present husband had adult children. Gwen was in full-time professional employment.

When Gwen came into therapy for problem gambling, she was very sceptical of the process. She had no first-hand experience of counselling or psychotherapy and told me early on that she was 'not someone to talk about myself . . . but I'm a good listener and I'm usually someone everyone else comes to.'

Gwen's situation at that stage was dire. She had been asked to leave by her husband when she had disclosed to him that she had been arrested for theft from the workplace, after handing herself in at the police station. Her place of work was in the care industry, where part of her role was, as she said, to be a very good listener. She had enjoyed her job; she felt that the caring aspect of her role, and the reward of helping others and making a difference to people's lives, fitted well with her personality and values.

Gambling at one stage was a regular activity for Gwen. She enjoyed buying the odd scratchcard or lottery ticket and, like many of us, she would dream of what she might do if ever she had a significant win. Her dreams would usually centre on how she might do something positive to change the lives of those she was close to, such as her friends and large family.

When the management at her place of work changed, so did Gwen's pattern of gambling. Having at that time recently suffered the sudden death of her mother, she felt particularly vulnerable to the excessive criticism of her new male boss. This was difficult for her because she had always taken an immense pride in applying herself to learning all there was to know and doing the best job she could, whatever her employment. There was an additional reason for her difficulty in working with her bullying male manager. Her former husband had been an alcoholic, who had subjected her to severe physical abuse from very early on in their marriage. Gwen took comfort from the fact that she had managed to find the courage to leave him after two years of marriage, vowing never to let a man treat her badly again.

Gwen's financial situation meant that she felt unable to leave her job, and did her best to manage her increasingly difficult working environment. Her manager's unfair treatment of her continued; she found it difficult to remain silent, but felt afraid of the consequences of putting in a complaint.

Gwen found herself lucky enough to have a couple of large scratchcard wins, and she began to think how different her life could be if she could just win enough to leave her job, and take time to look for alternative employment. Her luck seemed to be in, so she began to buy a few more cards than usual. On reflection, she says she felt hardly aware that each week her scratchcard spending was increasing, until one week she received a letter from her bank informing her that bills had been returned unpaid. Too ashamed to ask for her husband's help, she remembered the petty cash at work and thought that, if she just borrowed £100 and bought another few cards, she might win enough money to pay the bills before her husband found out they were unpaid. There was no win, and Gwen felt her anxiety rising.

Gwen's view of scratchcards as offering the hope of changing a life circumstance is a common one. Lotteries of course can offer the same chance, and on a grander scale, but the odds are against being a winner. Scratchcards offer a realistic possibility of a significant, if more modest, life change. Enough to perhaps send a friend having a tough time on holiday, or pay off a family member's credit card. The abusive relationship with her ex-husband had left Gwen wanting to rescue others she cared for from situations where they might be vulnerable, because she could imagine all too clearly how they might be feeling.

Scratchcards also offer an instant win, an instant solution to problems that might be resolved by money. This we can see was tempting to Gwen, when it came to the point at which she felt a sense of urgency at first to change her working situation, and then, later, the situation caused by the overbuying of scratchcards and the theft from petty cash. It is interesting to note that the thinking behind what Gwen describes as 'borrowing' money is frequently experienced by men or women who gamble problematically. It is a genuine belief, at the time, that the money will be returned when the hoped-for win materialises. This rarely happens, because either the win does not happen, or, if it does, the money is spent on further gambling, either in the hope of winning a little more or, more often, just to get more of the gambling experience, to escape the anxiety or lift the low mood that will often be more or less constant at that stage.

Gwen's experience of an abusive relationship had left her consciously determined never to be bullied by a man again. However, when she felt once again trapped in an abusive situation of a different kind at work, it brought up feelings connected to the original experience and she felt anxious, fearful and disempowered. She was ashamed of feeling vulnerable, and it was important to prove to herself that she could sort out the situation herself, because she felt that her manager would have 'won' if she had to enlist help via a complaint, or confiding in her husband. Gambling to win money was at first a way of her taking control of the situation, even if trusting to luck, rather than to other people.

We can hear how it did not take long for the sense of taking control and attempting to effect change by gambling to be lost, leaving Gwen more out of control and stuck than ever before. She confided that she had felt terrified at that time, and riddled with guilt, not only for the money that she had stolen, but more for lying to her husband, who was supportive and kind. By this time she felt unrecognisable to herself. In part, she was afraid of being caught having stolen, and having to reveal the extent of her problem. In part, she wished it would all be discovered, and that she would be made to stop, because she felt that she could not find the courage by herself to stand still and face the truth of her situation.

Chapter 5

Rock bottom

A recent interview with biologist Robert Trivers, published in the *New Scientist* magazine, explored the concept of deception, including self-deception. It discussed the reasons we lie, and gave the example of an extramarital affair. When in that situation, we lie to protect the relationship from judgement and criticism of others, who might not understand, or who might threaten the continuation of the affair (Lawton, 2011). We protect it because it makes us feel good; it makes us feel better about ourselves, and our lives.

The sense of being 'in' love is very much like that of being 'in' another world. The feelings we have transcend day-to-day life and problems, and we feel a sense of renewal, and hope. At times when we are not with our lover, memories of past meetings, and anticipation of the next, preoccupy us, and take the edge off the reality of life; and indeed off any of the shortcomings of our lover, or our relationship. We lie to ourselves to avoid any truth that might challenge the validity of what we have. Filled with the drug-like effect, we cannot imagine how we managed life before we had our lover, and the feelings they evoke. We may become highly anxious if threatened by the loss of the relationship, aware that without it we will face loss, pain and, by comparison, a flat, empty world. Often we go to almost any lengths to protect the relationship, and so to protect ourselves from pain.

Were we to swap the words relating to a love affair for those associated with problem gambling, the previous paragraph would be a description of the relationship with gambling, which would resonate with most women. Both types of relationship are transforming, seeming to meet needs for emotional management and to ease loneliness, depression and anxiety. Both can also then aggravate the very symptoms they seemed to alleviate. Just like any of us when we are in love, the woman is experiencing the rewarding feeling of being infused with the hormone dopamine. Her relationship with gambling may be devoid of the other rewards associated with romantic love, such as the physical presence of another, sexual gratification, or intimate psychological or emotional connection, but in terms of being rewarded by feeling good – albeit in the short term – the analogy of being 'in love' with the gambling activity might appropriately be used. And in just the same way that the other woman, desperately and blindly in love with her illicit lover, might lie to conceal and so maintain her relationship, the woman who is gambling will deceive others to conceal her activity, to protect and maintain her relationship with it. And, just as I am sure so many of us will recognise, if we continue with the parallel between a love relationship and problem gambling, she will also often deceive herself.

Denial in problem gambling (as with any addiction) is a mechanism by which the woman who is gambling, and who is so deeply involved in her relationship with gambling that she cannot imagine a way out, avoids looking at the reality of the damage that her behaviour is doing. She does so to justify to herself maintaining her relationship with gambling, and the perceived benefits that come with it. This is because she does not feel ready or able to let go of gambling. Often, we deny the existence of a problem until we believe we have the resources not only to face it but also to make positive changes.

Let us continue with the analogy with problem gambling and being involved in a dysfunctional love relationship. Perhaps we have all, with the benefit of hindsight, wondered how we could possibly not have seen that the negative relationship we were caught up in gave us predominantly pain and anxiety. How could we not have realised that, no matter how long we hung on in there, we would never get the ultimate result we wanted – the 'big win'. Perhaps we managed to deny ourselves the full reality, because to face the truth would mean we would have to consider ending the relationship? We would have to face the loss and pain that goes with the letting go; and feel foolish and ashamed, and angry with ourselves at having wasted our time and humiliated ourselves – again, all the same reasons why a woman who is gambling to excess lies to herself. The truth feels intolerable.

I have found that, if a woman is struggling to make sense of her gambling problem and why on earth she keeps going back to it, she will understand the dynamics more if we relate her situation to the difficulties involved in letting go of a relationship with someone loved. Most women who develop an addiction of any kind, and no less with gambling, have issues around rejection, inadequacy and loss in relationship. When their relationship with gambling begins to fail, these issues can be replayed. A favourite slot machine no longer paying out can feel like a personal rejection, a failing, unconsciously bringing up the pain of other rejections previously lived through. As they might have done in the relationship with another, they return to the machine, hoping to repair the situation, to prove themselves worthy. They are responding to inner messages, originally associated with relationships with parents or partners, which say:

> I've done something wrong, it must be my fault.

> When I did this before, it paid out (they loved me). Why won't it work now . . . ?

Women often remark that letting go of gambling feels so much harder than letting go of drugs or alcohol. I believe that a reason for this lies in that gambling creates more of this sense of a love relationship than drugs or alcohol. Although all three behaviours can create a numbing of the senses at the time of engagement, with gambling the process before, and after, is perhaps more active than with other addictions. There is often more to directly engage and connect with. In female problem gambling, there is most often an object to connect with: a slot machine, a computer screen. Money, of course, has a strong association with gambling, and is a reminder that has to be encountered daily.

Even when no longer engaged in the action of gambling, the experience is played out in the mind. Memories and images of gambling, the engagement with it, the wins, the venues visited, are active in the mind, as we might think of our time with a lover, when not in their presence. We know that images are a powerful aid to memory, and these memories make the grieving process during recovery a longer and more painful one. Carrying images of gambling in the mind makes for a powerful connection. Stopping the behaviour is one thing, stopping the thoughts and images that have taken up space in the mind for so long, often many years, quite another. Gambling is altogether a visceral experience.

By the stage we left both Claire and Gwen, they felt themselves to be on a roller coaster of emotion – with any time spent gambling releasing dopamine; complete absorption in the activity blocking out unwelcome thoughts and feelings; playing slot machines or buying scratch cards until all money spent; and losses and debt building. Here and now life was increasingly becoming a difficult zone to occupy, with anxiety creating adrenalin, which in turn produced more anxiety; then a craving for more of the gambling experience in the hope of feeling okay again.

By now, rational thought is hugely difficult, if not almost impossible. Considered responses are replaced by knee-jerk reactions to an increasingly desperate crisis. Somewhere, within herself, despite, and because of, the devastation caused by gambling, the woman is still pulled back to the same behaviour that once brought her a reward in terms of feeling better, even if only for a short while. And so she returns again and again to gamble. Repetitive gambling and its emotional, psychological and financial consequences have left her too confused and drained to do anything else – lacking in energy and motivation to try an alternative, lacking in belief that she could ever now cope without gambling, lacking in enough self-esteem to ask for help.

It is not at all unusual to hear women describe how by this time they no longer get any enjoyment at all from gambling. The reward, however they once experienced it, is no longer there. And yet, they still feel unmanageable cravings to repeat the behaviour. A significant reason for this is sheer disbelief that the reward won't return at some point. A woman has been so conditioned to expect it, and cannot face the disappointment that it may be gone for ever. Belief that she is unable to bear the sense of loss of the relationship she has with gambling is another reason for remaining hooked in. In a similar way that we might still miss a partner who has given us for some time nothing but heartache and a life of uncertainty, she knows that she will miss and grieve for her relationship with gambling – that giving it up will leave a void in her life, and that in that space it will be very difficult to continue to deceive herself about the mess that her gambling has made, and her part in allowing that to happen. And, of course, for the many women who gamble for escapism, it will be very hard to deny the existence of the problems that were the trigger for the onset of problem gambling. All this to face, when she is now, as a result of gambling to excess, in all likelihood weaker on all levels of her being than she has ever been before. Plus, we must remember, one of the factors that distinguishes gambling from other forms of addiction is that there is almost always a crushing financial impact of the behaviour to be faced and the hope that one more play could turn that around.

On paper, I am certain we can all see that it would make rational sense to stop gambling and face the truth. Do what needs to be done. I do hope, however, that we can also understand, or begin to have empathy for the reality of how, in a felt sense, this seems to the woman concerned impossible.

The reality, however, is that, despite our exploring how impossible it may feel, and how undoubtedly difficult it is to achieve, *women in the most extreme situations do stop excessive gambling.*

Let us hear more stories of how Claire and Gwen came to the point where they found enough strength within themselves to begin to want to take steps to break off their destructive relationship with gambling.

Claire

When we left Claire in the last chapter, she was trapped in the role of carer not only for her daughter but also for her mother. Gambling had become her escapism, and eventually began to feel like a life sentence. At times, when she did attempt to stop gambling, she found that her bulimia would be triggered.

When I asked Claire during one therapy session how she felt when she had eaten herself full of the sugary foods and drinks that she craved, she lay back in her chair, breathed out heavily, letting her arms fall loosely to her side. She looked relaxed and content. She was illustrating to me the deep level of satisfaction and relaxation that she felt, as a reward for overeating, despite the fact that she knew this was a fleeting feel-good moment, because it would be followed by regret and vomiting, self-loathing and shame, replicating the pattern she found herself in with gambling. Earlier in this chapter, we touched on the release of the hormone dopamine in encouraging the repetition of gambling behaviour, because it is connected with pleasure. Dopamine has also been found to have associations with eating. This is interesting because a high proportion of women I have seen in treatment for problem gambling also have or have had eating disorders. We will explore this connection in more detail when we look at the issue of cross-addiction in later chapters.

Clare's relationship with her daughter deteriorated. By the time she was 17 years old she had become increasingly violent towards her. Her mother remained demanding of Claire and also became verbally abusive. This served only to drive her to gambling.

When we are in traps, we seek any way out that we can. Claire could see no way out. To put healthy boundaries around her relationship with her daughter and her mother did not feel like an option. All she knew was the role of carer, and she felt too guilty to contemplate doing anything other than caring. The more she gambled, the more she felt she had to compensate for her behaviour by more caring.

To Claire, to stop gambling meant a return to overeating and hating herself all over again. She described to me one particularly bad morning. She had gambled for six hours the night before, lost all her money and arrived home to find her daughter missing. Claire was, that morning, feeling as low as she could ever remember feeling, riddled with guilt, deeply ashamed, sickened by gambling, and by herself and what she perceived as her weakness and stupidity in being unable to stop. She noticed a bottle of sleeping pills in the bathroom cabinet and, as she held them in her hand, she experienced a moment of stillness as she thought that here was a way out. If she took her own life, it would finally all stop. She told me how much that moment had scared her – that her gambling had brought her so much emotional agony that she could take comfort in the thought of her death. In that moment, fear that she had the potential to take her own life outweighed her fear of how she might cope without gambling. It was the window of clarity that she needed, and the motivation that she needed to become aware that she wanted to try once more to stop the downward spiral of gambling, and to seek support to do so.

Gwen

Gwen we left at the point of having stolen money from petty cash at work, in a desperate attempt to finance her gambling. She was falling deeper into debt with each week that went by, and found that, despite her conscious decision to borrow the money from work and replace it before anyone discovered it had gone, this did not happen. She later was to describe to me how she found that her luck with the scratchcards had 'run out': the wins stopped coming or, when they did come, there never seemed to be enough to make any difference to her debts, and so she would re-invest the money in more cards.

One of the hooks for Gwen's continuing was the 'near win' factor. If it seemed as if she had been just a moment away from a significant win, this would motivate her to buy more cards. Again, we see the power of hope at work, and how even for Gwen, who would describe herself as usually being a down-to-earth person, who was practical and dealt with facts, it felt easier to hang on to hope than to face the truth of the situation she now found herself in.

Gwen found that not only was her gambling affecting her finances, but also that her relationship with her second husband was beginning to suffer. She became preoccupied, withdrawn and secretive. As well as directly hiding her gambling, she was beginning to avoid discussing work, or how she spent her day in general, because she was afraid that any conversation might take her a step nearer to having her secret discovered. Soon, her home life too began to feel unpleasant and, in her by now confused thinking process she rationalised that, if she could just win enough money to pay back what she owed, all would be okay, she would stop gambling and life would return to normal.

There was by now over £2,000 to pay back at work. Gwen had gradually taken more and more money. The more she had taken, the less difference returning some of it seemed to make. She held out for the big, life-changing win. Her credit cards were at the limit and her monthly salary no longer took her bank account out of debit. Her anxiety about the money being discovered missing was growing and, in direct proportion to her growing anxiety, her capacity for logical thinking diminished. Fear freezes, and renders us feeling incapable of making sound decisions or doing anything other than acting on instinct and repeating familiar behaviour. With Gwen's background of domestic violence, too, although she might have known logically that her husband would offer her care and support to make positive changes, she was by this time in a constant state of fear, and vulnerability, as she had been during her first marriage, and so unconsciously she was wary of trusting in her present husband's reaction.

Gwen's 'rock bottom' came when the accountant in her workplace discovered discrepancies in the accounts. Gwen describes that moment as a huge relief, because it forced choice and change. As she phrased it, 'I needed to be dragged out of the tunnel, or I might never have come out.' Although she had not been accused of taking the money, she went directly to her local police station and handed herself in, reporting her theft. On returning home, she revealed everything to her husband, who was shocked and tearful and asked her to move out of their home while he had time to come to terms with the reality. She would later often describe in one-to-one therapy and in groups that for her, rock bottom was witnessing the look of hurt and distress on her husband's face when she disclosed everything to him. For her, seeing on his face the pain that her gambling had caused was the huge crash down to reality that she needed, but at the same time had been so afraid of experiencing. She maintained that, if ever again she felt at the point of deceiving herself that gambling might be a positive experience for her, the memory of her husband's face would be the reality check she needed. On leaving their home as he had asked, she sat in her car and made her first telephone call to a problem gambling treatment service, to ask for help.

We have heard just two examples of women reaching the point of wanting to take steps towards letting go of problem gambling. For both Claire and Gwen, rock bottom came when they experienced at emotional depth the consequences of their excessive gambling. This provided a window of reality just big enough to shed light on what was truly happening. Reaching this point is acutely painful and frightening, because not only does it mean facing the reality of the devastation gambling has often caused by this stage, but also taking a step closer to the reality of needing to let go of it. And let us always remember that, although gambling has caused this level of devastation, it has also been a perceived way of coping and/or escaping from a situation that initially almost always felt more damaging. When so much time and emotional and financial investment has been made in the gambling activity, it is going to take something considerable for it to seem as though the benefits of stopping outweigh the perceived benefits of continuing to gamble.

In the world of addiction, there is often talk of how someone needs to stop gambling for *themselves*, not for others. I think that the element of truth lies in the fact that the person with the problem needs to experience *consequences* for themselves. We have just touched on how the pain of withdrawal, and the crash into reality, is acute, so at some point the pain of continuing to gamble has to be experienced as greater than that of stopping. If we think of Gwen's rock bottom, it might seem as though she was stopping for her husband, but, if we think a level deeper, what she experienced at witnessing her husband's pain was a profound sense of guilt and pain of her own. It was as if her husband's expression mirrored to her the misery of her situation, which in that moment was greater than her fear of stopping and confronting the reality of her excessive gambling.

For both Gwen and Claire we see that their rock bottom was like a snapshot in time, a moment of clarity, which brought about subjectively their own desire for change. Rock bottom may not be a permanent state, or indeed be long-lasting, if and when it is reached. Often have I heard a woman swear to herself, others and me that 'this is it, I cannot allow myself to go through this again, I have to stop', only to find that, despite her best intentions, triggers to gamble arise, cravings win out and relapse occurs, especially so without support. Sometimes a few rock bottoms need to be reached before, if I may quote the Gamblers Anonymous meetings, she is 'sick and tired of feeling sick and tired'.

What Claire and Gwen also show us is that rock bottom does not have to mean losing everything. Yes, for some it might mean that jobs, homes and relationships are lost before there is any desire for positive change. And again, even then there is no guarantee that this will create enough motivation for problematic gambling to be stopped. I worked with one woman who would regularly speak of the torment she had suffered following another gambling binge that she had sworn to herself she would never have, describing how she returned from the casino slot machines physically shaking, nauseous, unable to force down food or to sleep; racked with shame, and guilt at time spent away from her children, and her marriage, yet again on the point of physical collapse, caused by all money being lost. Each time she would swear to herself and to me that that had to be the last time. She could take no more of the pain she inflicted on herself by gambling. Each time she truly meant what she said. Yet each time too, the moment she stepped out of the therapy session and into the whirlwind of frantic activity and anxiety that was her life, back into the old patterns and old problems, the pattern of gambling would begin again too. There needed to be practical change, as well as intellectual resolve and emotional consequence.

How many of us take a holiday and, in that moment of stillness it provides, look at the reality of our lives? We cannot deny we work too hard, drink too much, see too little of our friends, and so we swear to ourselves when we get back home that we will make changes. And how many of us do? The reason is often that we get swept up again, in fast-moving, familiar patterns, and start to do the same unhealthy things all over again . . . We need to keep focused on making the changes we want, and get into action as soon as we can in terms of new behaviour. Change is difficult and it always feels easier to do 'the same old same old'. It is really no different with withdrawal from addiction.

What *is* absolutely necessary, as a start, is that for a moment the woman with the gambling problem is unable to deny to herself that the benefits of becoming gambling free – however terrifying and difficult that thought might be – outweigh the perceived benefits of continuing to gamble. And this is usually measured in terms of emotional pain and psychological distress, rather than in monetary terms, even though of course extreme debt can bring about such distress, as we have seen from Gwen's case in particular. The next crucial step is towards actual change in behaviour patterns, ideally with professional support. We shall look at this further in Chapter 6 and beyond.

Women struggling with problematic gambling behaviour are notoriously in the minority when it comes to seeking treatment for the problem. Historically, their low numbers in the consulting room have been misinterpreted as meaning that few women have gambling problems. Not so. I know this from anecdotal evidence from women I have seen for problem gambling issues. They know how many others are out there who are not seeking help.

So, when a woman gets to the point of suffering at the level that we hear both Claire and Gwen were, what stops her seeking help?

Issues of shame and guilt, as we explored in earlier chapters, are important factors. In the past, it has been particularly hard to reveal oneself as a woman who gambles, whether socially or problematically, when it has been seen as a predominantly male activity. As we know, more recently, the issues of both female gambling and female problem gambling have been openly discussed in the media, and research has shown an increase in reported problematic female gambling (Gambling Commission, 2010). Yet still low numbers of women are reported as coming forward for treatment. So why is that? One primary reason I believe women do not hurry to seek treatment is that it might just work.

Ambivalence is normal, but women whose gambling is truly a dependency and a form of escape have a higher degree of ambivalence, because letting go of their perceived way of coping is extremely anxiety provoking. If a woman has a long-term gambling problem, there are deeply entrenched patterns of behaviour to change. She may have forgotten how life was without gambling, may have no positive frame of reference for coping with life and strong emotion without it, and so fear the change. Or, instead of fearing that treatment might work, she may be cynical of the idea that anything can help her to stop, particularly if she has made several failed attempts in the past.

If we bear in mind that gambling – like any addiction – damages relational skills, a woman may be fearful of the level of intimacy required to be with another in the therapeutic process and, if she has experienced domestic violence, or abuse, even more so.

For women who have children, a concern can be whether seeking treatment for problem gambling and all its related issues will lead to Social Services involvement, and risk the children being taken into care.

For women who have a mental health diagnosis, there may be concerns that seeking problem gambling treatment will mean their medication might be altered, or that reporting any depression, anxiety or suicidal thoughts might result in hospitalisation. Even those who do not have a mental health diagnosis may be concerned about whether their gambling will be recorded on medical records, if they register with a treatment agency, and how this might affect employment, or again reflect on their abilities to parent.

Practical issues can be problematic. Remember a woman is likely to be confused, in emotional turmoil and with her life in flux at the point of deciding to seek help. Concentrating on finding an appropriate treatment service can seem like a Herculean task at such a time. Many women report that they might have come forward sooner for counselling or therapy had they known of the existence of specialised services, especially those that offer services to meet the needs of women. This can be a particularly encouraging factor for the many women who have sensitive underlying issues.

Sometimes, sadly, the reason a woman does not come forward might just be that the moment is lost. The window of reality that shed light on the torment her gambling was causing, and motivated the will to change, closes again. This is more likely perhaps for the woman who lives alone, is isolated, or has concealed her gambling from those close to her. If there is only her to witness that moment of rock bottom, it is harder to maintain a level of motivation to begin the change process, and easier for her to slip back into deceiving herself once more, and to return to the gambling behaviour until, hopefully, there is a next time.

What we are seeing is that rock bottom is not the end of problematic gambling behaviour, but only the beginning of a complex process of change.

Chapter 6

Assessing reality

We have so far identified some key triggers for gambling to excess, we have seen how gambling turns from being a perceived coping mechanism and *rescuer* to a destructive behaviour that feels out of a woman's control, and seems to take on a life of its own, as her *persecutor*. She is caught up in a drama triangle, because she now feels a *victim* of her addiction (Orriss, 2004). We have seen that it feels easier to deny a lot of these issues than face painful reality. We have discussed excessive gambling as bringing about changes in a woman's behaviour and character that leave her unrecognisable to herself; how desperation leads her to behave in ways that are against her previous value system and moral code, as well as sometimes those of society. We understand that rock bottom, however it may be experienced by the individual, is not measured in financial terms, but in feeling emotional pain, psychological distress and often physical discomfort so great that it eventually outweighs what she feels are the benefits of continuing to gamble.

In Chapter 5, we noted the importance of not just an intellectual decision to change behaviour, borne out of the pain of being sick and tired of gambling, but *actioning* change at the earliest opportunity before the moment is lost under overwhelming cravings for further gambling. These are likely still to occur, even if a woman has made a rational decision to stop. Stopping is a process, it will take time and there are likely to be phases of relapse, as she come to terms with all that has happened during the period of her gambling, as well as whatever was happening before, which may have led to it. It is much easier for this to be worked through with professional support.

The woman who is fortunate enough to have a good support network of family and friends may feel that this will be adequate support to see her through. Family and friends are undoubtedly a potentially invaluable source of strength and motivation for change. As we have discussed, it makes a positive difference to have support and truly intimate relation-ships, but don't we often find it the hardest to be completely open and honest with those we are closest to? Aren't we afraid that what we say when revealing what we think of as our darkest secrets may make them sad, angry, cause them to judge and even reject us?

Sometimes, an unhealthy and stuck pattern of relating with family or friends may be contributing as a trigger to the gambling problem, with neither the woman who is gambling nor the other/s involved consciously aware of that. Neither side, without objective professional help, may be able to see the wood for the trees, and the same old patterns will continue to repeat themselves. This will make it difficult for lasting change to take place. It is not enough just to stop the gambling behaviour – adjustments need to be made to defuse whatever the triggers for it might be.

Another factor that is important to bear in mind is that the gambling problem also has an impact on those close to the woman concerned. Those who are aware of her problem may have been so intent on supporting her emotionally, bailing her out financially, feeling they were walking on egg shells for fear of triggering the problem, even though they did not know what had caused it, that they have put their own feelings and needs so far aside they have almost lost sight of them.

Those who were unaware of the woman's gambling until it was discovered, or she chose to disclose it, may be in shock, angry, feeling their world has been turned upside down. Who is this person they thought they knew? They often feel scared because gambling problem was so easily hidden; how can they be sure she has really stopped? Trust has been shattered. Indeed for them, the crash into reality can be just as traumatic as it is for the woman herself.

When feelings are understandably running high, thinking is confused and the effects of excessive gambling are having an impact on family and others close to the woman concerned, even with the best of intentions it will be impossible for all concerned to remain objective. This is not the healthiest situation for anyone, including the woman who is taking the first steps toward letting go of gambling. To give herself the best chance, she will need space to begin to be completely open and honest with herself about what she feels about her gambling and *what* it is – and yes, maybe even *who* it is – in life that she is finding so hard to cope with that she feels she needs to go to such great and ultimately destructive lengths to escape. Affected others often benefit from professional support to come to terms with what has happened, and as a way of understanding the basic psychology of problem gambling so as to help and support the woman with the problem in a way that is truly productive and helpful to recovery.

They can learn how to look after themselves and set healthy boundaries around the gambling behaviour, how to adjust unhealthy patterns of relating and how to identify ways that they might inadvertently have been enabling the woman to gamble. However, the thought of seeking professional support can be uncomfortable for affected others, who often wonder why they should seek help when it is not they who have the problem.

Let us focus once more on the woman with the gambling problem. The initial step of any sound professional support will involve a thorough assessment procedure. This is an opportunity for the women considering treatment to meet with a professional, for both parties to get an overview of her situation and to identify any expectations or concerns associated with the process. It is an initial meeting with, at that stage, no commitment on either side to contract to work regularly together. A bit like a two-way interview, in which both will work out if they think they will be able to work productively together.

Shall we for a moment consider what this experience might be like for the woman who takes this step? We know that by this time, whether or not she has family and friends, she has been used to living in the bubble of relative isolation created by her addiction. This has left her unused to any relational depth, or intimacy, certainly anything like the one-to-one attention she will receive at assessment. She is likely to be feeling ashamed of the lengths to which she has gone to hide her gambling problem, and she may have spent years in denial of the impact her gambling has had on herself, those around her and her life in general. She may still be reeling from her bubble being burst, and her sudden exposure to reality. She may feel ashamed of her physical appearance; her self-care may have begun to suffer. For example, I have seen several women who have not seen a dentist or a doctor for years, or bothered about their general personal appearance. They have been so caught up in gambling with racing thoughts, tumultuous emotions, lurching from crisis to crisis that their bodies and physical needs have been ignored. If a woman has committed illegal acts, she may have anxieties about what will happen if she discloses these at assessment. To summarise, she is likely to be fearful of the judgement of the professional. After all, how can she believe another person might be able to accept her when at this stage her self-acceptance is at an all-time low?

For the professional who is aware of these issues, assessment sensitively and skilfully handled is a chance to positively engage with the woman, and to perhaps give her first experience in some time (sadly, for some women, perhaps ever) of relating in an appropriately warm, productive way with another. It is likely that, if she has discussed anything in relation to her gambling problem before now, it will have been a catalyst for arguments and upset with those who perhaps do not understand how she could have become addicted to gambling, and told her just to stop wasting her money, that it doesn't make sense. This type of interaction has very likely motivated her to 'go underground' with her problem, and to distance herself from relationship. She may now be very sensitive and watchful for the same reaction in assessment. How encouraging it can feel to have an experience of a professional communicating that they understand how excessive gambling can be an escapism, that as with any addiction it can trigger behaviour that is not part of usual character, morals or values, and that they understand she is likely to be ambivalent regarding change. And, importantly of course, apart from the very few exceptions mentioned later in this chapter, what she discloses will remain confidential.

Communicating that ambivalence is normal, and does not have to be a block to beginning treatment, is a valuable intervention. Many women I have seen have believed that, if there is any part of them that still wants to gamble, that means they are not ready for change. If every woman with a gambling problem had to wait for the stage of having no doubts, or anxieties, about letting go of gambling, I think I would never have seen a client. It is normal to still crave gambling, even if a woman consciously wishes to stop. We will explore this in more depth later in this book.

Becoming free of problem gambling is a process through which the woman with the problem and the professional will work together. The sense of 'doing it together', and of assessment conveying that sense of collaboration, is essential. For the professional, the art of offering a collaborative working relationship is a balancing act, which is well worth investing the time and energy in thinking through, and developing as a key skill.

If a woman on her first meeting with a professional is given a message, either verbally or in the subtext, that it is all down to her, that she has to do all the work, it may tip the balance for her deciding not to commit to regular sessions. After all, why would she bother, if she thinks she has do it all by herself? She might as well stay home and do so. She is aware that coming in to regular counselling, or therapy sessions, is going to require an investment, financially, emotionally, psychologically and in time. She will naturally want to think she will get some return from this investment, in the shape of active engagement and support.

Some professionals fall into the pattern of thinking and communicating to the client that it is all down to them, because they view addiction as an ultimate act of irresponsibility, and therefore want to reverse that process very quickly, by communicating to the client, intentionally or unintentionally, that they need to take *all* responsibility for recovery from the word go.

> I didn't see how it was going to work. He just kept telling me he couldn't help me stop (gambling), that I had to do it myself. If I could do it by myself, I would have done it by now. I need to believe someone knows what it's like, and knows how to give me some guidance to get there. (Woman at assessment for an online gambling problem, commenting on previous therapy)

Yes, of course it is essential that a woman does begin to take responsibility for herself and her life, and to develop a more 'adult' sense of herself and her world. But let us remember that, in the grip of addiction and in the early phases of recovery, she feels controlled by her strong cravings for gambling and the uncomfortable emotions that trigger it, and so in that sense she is feeling *childlike*. She is likely to feel encouraged, contained and safe enough to continue with professional support if she feels a good sense that the person she is working with has an understanding of her issues, and is able to offer her practical suggestions and strategies to limit and stop her problematic gambling, as well as an outline of what to expect from the process:

Having said what I have previously, this should not be taken as my suggesting that at assessment the professional is overly prescriptive and directive, and does all the work. Let us remember that, often, gambling becomes problematic for women because they are feeling out of control of certain aspects of their lives, and of their emotional world. To feel that the professional is attempting to take control can be perceived as threatening, especially for the woman who has experienced abuse or domestic violence. She in particular will be very watchful for signs that the professional might abuse their position of power. For that is how the professional with be seen through her eyes – a powerful authority figure. As a result, she will transfer her past experiences of authority figures onto them, and somewhere within herself expect a similar pattern of treatment that she may have received from those who had power over her previously. It is therefore valuable and reassuring if the professional communicates awareness of appropriate boundaries, resilience and professional experience, but that the ultimate decision about committing to regular professional help, and the depth at which to explore sensitive issues, rests with the woman concerned:

I didn't go back after the first session, she (the counsellor) hardly looked at me, just kept writing on a clipboard and asking me about the sexual abuse, and I had told her I didn't want to talk about that. It's too upsetting and I didn't feel comfortable.' (40-year-old woman, gambling on slot machines, at assessment for one-to-one therapy)

So, here we are with what perhaps seem like suggestions for a way of being for professionals at assessment, based on my experience, that are in some ways contradictory and may seem an almost impossible balance to achieve. I think, however, most important of all in the initial assessment is to watch, and to listen, and to make a connection with the individual woman there in the consulting room; not to be blinded by the label 'problem gambler', which might sometimes get stuck over our eyes, as professionals. Along with that, the fear that dealing with addiction often builds up in those unused to working with it prevents their seeing what is really going on around and underneath the gambling behaviour. The woman with the problem will be encouraged, if she is able to see and hear, that she is being seen and heard as more than 'a gambler', with her behaviour having a meaning rather than meaningless self-destruction, because she may have forgotten, or still be unaware of, this herself. Often this experience is enough to motivate her to commit to regular support.

I wish to emphasise, however, that it is important too to pay attention to the specifics of the gambling behaviour. After all, that is the problem with which the woman is presenting and wants to resolve. The *DSM-1V* (American Psychiatric Association, 2005) is widely used by mental health professionals in the USA, and other countries including the UK, in order to make psychiatric diagnoses. The *DSM-IV* classifies problem gambling as an impulse control disorder, rather than an addiction (p. 618), but here I say this more for information's sake. The symptoms of problem gambling – as we have discussed so far – appear similar to those of many other forms of recognised addiction, and certainly feel like addiction to the person caught up in them. So does the often acute pain of withdrawal.

I realise that when I mention the notions of categorisation, screens and assessment, I risk losing some readers, because many will be horrified at the thought of these. Others might think that I have 'sold out', because have I not spent much of this book so far talking of the importance of the *meaning* of gambling, and seeing the woman underneath the behavioural symptoms? Yet, a positive of the *DSM-1V* is that it does focus on the psychological motivation of problem gambling. If used well, and with sensitivity to the individual, it can form an entire conversation at assessment. If we take a look at the *DSM-IV* assessment that follows, we will recognise many of the issues we have already come across in this book in case studies and discussion.

The *DSM-IV* screening checklist has the following ten questions:

1. Are you preoccupied with gambling (e.g. preoccupied with reliving past gambling experiences, handicapping or planning the next venture, or thinking of ways to get money with which to gamble)?
2. Do you need to gamble with increasing amounts of money in order to achieve the desired excitement?
3. Have you made repeated unsuccessful efforts to control, cut back, or stop gambling?
4. Are you restless or irritable when attempting to cut down or stop gambling?
5. Do you gamble as a way of escaping from problems or of relieving feelings of helplessness, guilt, anxiety, or depression?
6. After losing money gambling, do you often return another day to get even?
7. Do you lie to family members, therapists, or to others to conceal the extent of involvement with gambling?
8. Have you committed illegal acts such as forgery, fraud, theft, or embezzlement to finance gambling?
9. Have you jeopardized or lost a significant relationship, job or educational or career opportunity because of gambling?
10. Do you rely on others to provide money to relieve a desperate financial situation caused by gambling?

Answering yes to five or more of the questions on the *DSM-IV* indicates meeting the criteria for pathological gambling.

If a woman does not meet the criteria, and scores low on the *DSM-IV*, this does not necessarily indicate that she does not have a gambling problem. Often I have been asked, while in an initial assessment meeting, what do I think? For example, do I think the woman has a gambling problem after all, because she is not in debt and not spending all her money on the activity of gambling? I think, as we have identified, it is important not to focus exclusively on the amount of money spent and lost on gambling as the only indicator of a gambling problem. If the woman's finances are okay, yet gambling is a source of argument and is destabilising her relationships, her job, that may be enough to make her gambling a problem to her. Ultimately, if anything about her pattern of gambling is creating blocks to the kind of life she might want for herself, it is problematic gambling.

I strongly encourage wherever possible that the *DSM-IV* is completed in the room with both the woman seeking help and the professional present. Experience has shown that there is a missed opportunity to learn from her responses to the questions if paperwork is filled in remotely or while she is alone in the waiting area. As we see, the questions in the *DSM-IV* screen are a distillation of the painful, often shameful and anxiety-provoking issues that together form both the triggers and consequences of problem gambling. The woman at initial assessment, having been in denial of the extent of her problem, by hiding away in continued gambling, and perhaps only just beginning to face reality will find answering these questions to be like looking in a metaphorical mirror, and having reflected back 'The vision of a woman, wild with more than womanly despair' (Coleridge, 1896). This can have a value, because it can dispel any lingering self-deception regarding the impact of her gambling on herself and those around her, and so encourage and increase her motivation to stop. The supportive professional might be creative and tentatively encourage further discussion around each question.

For example:

Q1.   If she answers 'yes', and then 'yes' to question 5, it is clear that escapism is what she is craving from her gambling experience.

Q2.   This might be reframed, to ask whether she is gambling with increased amounts of money in order to *get whatever experience she feels she needs from gambling* (remembering that many women do not gamble with excitement as the aim, but more to achieve a sense of emotional numbness).

Q3.   Be specific. If 'yes', has she received professional support before, or attended Gamblers Anonymous meetings? This is a chance to discover what has proved helpful and was has proved unhelpful, and why.

Q4.   She may not have made deliberate attempts to stop. But, if she had no money to gamble, or could not physically get to do so, how did she feel? This question refers to withdrawal symptoms. It can be a good opening for discussion of the fact that withdrawal from problem gambling is every bit as real, and to be taken as seriously as, withdrawal from drugs or alcohol. Something she may not understand or allow herself to understand, because she feels less entitled to struggle in withdrawal when she is not putting drugs or alcohol into her system.

Q5.   Does she notice what particular feelings seem the most difficult to cope with?

Q6.   If she wins, can she walk away with that money? Or will she tend to buy further gambling time with winnings?

Q7.   If she has lied to others close to her to conceal her problem, it might be useful to ask what is it like to be honest about it there in that moment with a stranger?

Q8.   Remember, this may bring up particular anxieties around what will happen if she answers 'yes'. This is a useful point at which to clarify limits to confidentiality, including those around child protection, if appropriate.

Q9.   Does she want to say a little more about how her relationships have been affected?

Q10.   Does she still owe money to family and friends? Many women find the guilt of owing £10 to a friend a greater pressure than owing £1,000 to the bank. And the discomfort of guilt can be a trigger for further gambling.

There are other reasons I would suggest that any gambling screens are conducted with the professional present and active in the process. We know, too, that as well as to allow herself to hold on to the escapism of gambling that she feels she needs, a woman's denial has been about avoiding the pain of an ever-worsening reality. If the assessment is completed with an experienced professional, she has available the support she needs if emotionally overwhelmed. At these times, the skilled and sensitive professional will acknowledge and reflect that the questions are provoking an intolerable level of psychological and emotional distress, and either limit exploration around each question, stick just to the questions, or abandon them in their structured form altogether, the priority always being the well-being of the woman and the fragile and fledgling working relationship.

Because assessment is the beginning of the reversal of the process of excessive gambling – facilitating expression, rather than suppression – it is not unusual for a woman to have urges to gamble on leaving the assessment, and in some cases to do just that. After all, her excessive gambling has done a good job of covering up painful thoughts and feelings, and an initial assessment begins to uncover them. To introduce the idea that increased gambling urges often arise after initial assessment and to explain why, and that it is a normal part of the process, can be a very useful way to encourage a return for regular sessions. If it is not mentioned, and gambling does occur as a result of unsettling thoughts and feelings evoked during assessment, an association can be developed with professional support making things worse, and so constructing a barrier to return, or for the woman to seek alternative support in the future. Encouraging her to look after herself when she leaves the session begins to introduce the idea of self-care, that she is of value, and that her thoughts and feelings are to be taken seriously. This may be a new concept to her since her gambling took over, because she is likely to be more used to self-deprecation than self-care. It might also be an appropriate time to introduce the idea that it is possible to use coping mechanisms if urges do arise. We will look at these in later chapters.

By the assessment stage, many women are aware that their gambling is a coping mechanism. They may be reluctant to reveal this because they feel it portrays them as being vulnerable, or they may fear revealing in assessment the issue or issues that they are using gambling to escape from, because these are often intimate and sensitive. My experience is that women who are using gambling as escapism know they are doing so more often than do male clients. Many women present with histories of cross-addiction, which indicates that the issue they are attempting to cope with, via a pattern of addiction to one thing or another, has not been addressed, or possibly even identified. The causal root of a woman's pattern of addiction is more often than not one and the same, even if there are several shoots growing off the root, in the form of drugs, alcohol, self-harm, eating disorder and problem gambling. If she can find a model of counselling or therapy that will not only help her to make behavioural change but will also enable her to take long enough to look at her whole self, and life history, to trace the origins of the pattern of managing emotion and disturbing thoughts by escapism, it can be just what she needs to break the cycle.

Since the availability of online gambling, and the rapidity of play taking some women by surprise, it has increased the likelihood that some women may present for help, not having gambled for escape but having slipped swiftly down the scale from social or regular gambling to problem gambling. This happened because they lost more money than they could afford, and they have fallen into the downward spiral of loss chasing. If so, their primary problem might well be their financial crisis, and they may not need long-term counselling or therapy. Shorter term, more behavioural-focused work such as cognitive behavioural therapy (CBT) may prove enough to get to grips with the cravings to gamble to win back lost money, and to come to terms with what they feel in the aftermath of the crisis.

As with any initial assessment for any professional help, it is appropriate and ethical that details are taken of any physical health problems and mental health problems, including history of suicide attempts, or any current thoughts of this. Suicidal *thoughts* are not uncommon when problem gambling has reached crisis point but, if there is *serious intention*, or a *plan* in place, it is necessary for professionals to consider whether it feels within their limitations and/or those of their service to work with these difficulties, and to offer regular treatment sessions. The needs of a very few women may not be adequately met within traditional counselling or psychotherapy methods. If there is reason to believe that there is *serious intention* of a woman doing serious harm to herself, or to another, it is preferable wherever possible to consult with her GP, or psychiatrist, or other mental health professional, if she is engaged with those services. Safety always has to take priority and no work can be done unless both she and the professional she has approached feel safe, within the establishing relationship. Transparency with the woman who is seeking support is always preferable in such circumstances, where other health professionals she is engaging with may need to be consulted. The same applies if, for reasons of child protection, confidentiality might need to be broken. This level of transparency promotes a sense of trust, and encourages the woman to engage with whichever service may be best able to offer her the appropriate support she needs.

If we move beyond the word 'assessment', with all its connotations of judgement, and put down for a moment the problem gambling screens, essentially and importantly, assessment is really a chance to meet, to see if two people are able to form a healthy working relationship together. If the professional can stay in touch with the reality that in addition to meeting the criteria for pathological gambling, the person seeking help is a woman going through a time of great despair, likely to be scared and confused, hoping the person she is meeting with, and sharing many sensitive details of her life with, can help her to help herself, it is already a good start, and the beginning of change. The creation of the possibility of engaging in a strong working *relationship* is the *most* important element at that meeting.

Chapter 7

Creating a therapeutic experience

In addiction, a person is never united and singularly determined in thought, feeling and action. The woman whose gambling is out of control is experiencing a complex inner battle with contradicting thoughts and feelings, resulting in behaviour that is often erratic and confusing to herself, as well as to those around her.

If we think about it, even when not caught in addiction, are we not to some degree or another often trying to resolve similar internal battles? The phrase 'I'm in two minds' illustrates that we are aware of the inner conflicts and contradictions we face when we are trying to resolve external dilemmas. We face these daily, when making a decision about whether to have the muffin or the apple at lunch, or with larger more important life decisions, such as whether to make a commitment to stay in a dull but secure job or take a risk on a new one. The reason we often find it so hard to make a decision or to know what the 'right thing' for us is – let alone to do it – is that we have more than one part of us making the decision at any one time.

Transactional Analysis (TA) is an integrative theory of personality and a systemic psychotherapy, containing elements of psychoanalytic, humanistic and cognitive approaches. The theory was developed by the US psychiatrist, Eric Berne, and began to be practised in the 1950s. TA uses the Parent, Adult, Child model to explain why we have complex inner dialogues between parts of ourselves that think and feel conflicting things. These then influence our subsequent behaviour patterns (Berne, 2010).

Outlined here is the adaptation of the TA model, which I use to explain these dynamics to clients in my therapeutic practice.

No matter how old, or wise, or powerful we become, we have the following inside of us:

The Child: this part of us can be freeing, creative and playful. Like most children, it can sometimes be rebellious too. And, like a child, it can get us into trouble if it has too much freedom. The Child is tuned towards, and reacts to, our strong feelings and emotions about the decision we are trying to make. Whenever we are experiencing emotions that seem beyond our control, it is a good indication that our Child feels like the strongest part of us at that time.

The Parent: this part of us we might imagine as an internal recording device, beginning to record information from the moment we have an awareness of the existence of others, and that it is in our best interests to please them if we are going to survive. So, it records all the things we were told we 'should always' do, and all the things we were told we 'should never' do. It is not just recording verbal messages, but it has an invisible video-recording function, too. It records not only what we are told we should do to 'Be good', but examples of behaviour we witnessed in people with authority and power over us – not only our parents, but also grandparents, teachers and elders. These include society's norms and values. So, from our first conscious existence, this part of us not only records verbal and visual messages but also forms our 'script' for how we 'should' and 'ought to' live our lives.

The Adult: this part of us is rational, capable of looking at the available facts and information from both Parent and Child, weighing it all up, and then making the best and healthiest decision based on that information.

It is good and healthy that we have a well-functioning Parent. It can stop us from doing things that might harm us, like walking out in front of traffic, or eating the entire box of chocolates all at once, and so feeling sick afterwards. If, however, the volume on the recording of rules for how to live our life is too loud, it can drown out other messages about what we truly want for ourselves. As adults, we can end up living an unhappily inauthentic life, because we are living it by the values and morals that may have suited our parents or other authority figures but may not suit us.

In the world of problem gambling treatment, there are various schools of thought as to which treatment is most effective. Experience has taught me that forms of treatment that take into account, and offer explanation for, the internal conflicts we wrestle with are essential. It can be a scary thing to feel that, despite the very best conscious intentions to stop gambling, there is another part of a woman that will drag her back to the behaviour that she is rationally aware is destroying her, but paradoxically feels she needs so desperately. Sometimes women have very tentatively spoken of this experience as:

It's like I have a split personality.

I'm not saying I'm schizophrenic, but it's like I'm two people and another part of me just takes over and I just end up there (the amusement arcade).

To understand the concept that we are not just one whole, one set of consistent and matching thoughts, feelings and desires is not only comforting but empowering. It shows a woman that her gambling does not 'just happen'. Gambling behaviour happens because she might in her Adult have made the decision to stop, but strong feelings and reactions from the Child, and loud messages from the Parent, are likely to be interfering with her decision, and the conflicts between all three making the whole process so difficult. If she can begin to learn as much as she can about herself, she will be more aware of what drives the problematic gambling, and, too, what it is that she needs to go on to develop a healthy and productive lifestyle, making relapse or cross-addiction less likely. And this she may discover is very different from the life she has been leading, if she has been living it exclusively according to the rules of the Parent, never having stopped to edit the recording.

The woman can learn how to strengthen her Adult through information on what triggers her gambling, and what it is that the Child feels is so horribly scary and painful that that part of her wants to escape into the safety of gambling. She can learn what rules from the Parent she feels she has broken, and so punishes herself after gambling, rather than trying to understand the behaviour and to learn from the relapse.

Eventually, the woman can learn how to have a working relationship with all parts of herself.

TA uses the term 'injunctions' for the set of 12 rules, which we may record and live our lives by. For the purpose of this book, after describing the injunctions, I will then refer to them as 'rules', because this is the term I most often use with clients.

As the rules are predominantly learnt when we are children, no matter how old we are now, if we do as the rules tell us, we feel we are being good, and so believe everything will be okay. If we do not obey the rules, we feel we are bad, and fear disapproval or punishment, which we might have learnt to receive, or were threatened with, when children.

TA identifies the following injunctions:

1. Don't be.
2. Don't be who you are.
3. Don't be a child.
4. Don't grow up.
5. Don't succeed.
6. Don't do anything.
7. Don't be important.
8. Don't belong.
9. Don't be close.
10. Don't be well (don't be sane).
11. Don't think.
12. Don't feel.

Along with these injunctions (rules), TA identifies six 'drivers', which influence our thoughts, feelings and behaviour:

1. Please others.
2. Be perfect.
3. Be strong.
4. Work hard.
5. Hurry up.
6. Be careful.

Concentrating again on the woman who gambles, I have always found these rules and drivers to be significant factors in triggering her gambling. I have found too, that certain rules and drivers are reasons for histories of cross-addiction and comorbidity (eating disorder, self-harming behaviour) because these behaviours often too prove to be coping mechanisms or ways of dealing with emotional distress.

The reason that the rules have been at least contributory triggers is that living life according to any one, and sometimes several, of the 12 has left the woman who gambles overwhelmed with external and internal pressure to perform and conform. She is living life driven by unconscious child-hood fears of what will happen if she does not obey the rules. She lives, at best, a life that does not feel true to herself, and so takes an escape route via gambling to switch off from the pressures and the nagging voices driving her from within. If bad things have happened along the way, 'Don't be close' and/or 'Be strong', for example, may have been blocks to her seeking help and support.

The rules and drivers also continue to drive the gambling behaviour, and later relapse, because each time the woman slips and gambles again, she feels she has broken a rule. The Child feels that gambling breaks the rule of 'Be strong', 'Be perfect', or 'Please others'. Therefore, the Child feels she must deserve a punishment. Telling herself this and punishing herself for long enough drives her to return to gambling, to escape the anxiety and depression that inevitably result.

Learning about one's own particular recording of rules and drivers, and doing a little editing, will help. None of us are able to wipe the recording clean but, once aware of what is on it, it is often easier to find the volume control and turn it down, so that we can then hear the expression of our own more authentic needs and wants.

I have found one of the additional values of TA to be in its user friendliness. The basic concepts are easy to explain, and indeed easy enough to illustrate. Several members in the women's groups I have facilitated have been enlightened – and amused – when subjected to my flip chart stick man (or woman . . . ?) Parent, Adult, Child drawings, and felt that they have helped them to understand their split and ambivalent thoughts and feelings, which I now illustrate:

- The Adult makes a healthy decision, based on all the information to hand that the logical thing is to stop gambling.
- The Child stick person, at some point, feels scared by something that brings up feelings that seem unmanageable (as they often do when we are children), and so runs to hide in the safe place of gambling.
- The Parent, after the gambling episode, then tells off the Child, and, depending on real childhood life experiences of authority figures, repeats messages that provoke feelings of guilt, shame and generally feeling bad.
- The Child then wants to run back to gambling, to escape from the critical parent messages.

For the woman who is not just dealing with her own inner Parent, but is herself a parent, the perceived intolerable guilt she may feel at having gambled, and so deprived her children of material resources, time and attention, adds to the guilt and shame from the inner Parent messages, thereby triggering further gambling. It is valuable learning that there are times when, even though physically she is a parent and a adult, there are *reasons* for her being pulled into her gambling behaviour, and often that is because she is feeling childlike and scared herself. This helps her to develop a compassionate attitude toward herself. This then turns down the volume on the critical Parent recording, with its expectations of punishment, and so helps to break the cycle of relapse.

In my practice, I integrate elements of Cognitive Behavioural Therapy (CBT). If used as an undiluted therapeutic model, it has a focus mainly on behavioural change. This may have a value, as I mentioned earlier, for those women who are now coming forward for help having slipped down the spectrum of gambling from social to problematic, often being caught out by the rapidity of play and drawn into a cycle of loss chasing. CBT, which focuses on what we think, how those thoughts affect our emotional state and how we then behave as a result of that process, aims to help a client see a link between negative thoughts and negative mood, and thereby gain control over negative emotions and change behaviour. CBT pays particular attention to the here and now, and does not concentrate on finding the causes of emotional distress. CBT therapists often suggest 'homework' for clients, such as keeping a diary with observations on thoughts, or practising behaving in a certain way to work toward change in behavioural patterns.

The CBT model is highly effective, based on available evidence. However, used exclusively with women such as those we have discussed, who have deeply troubling issues underlying their gambling problem, it may have limited effect. I have clients who have reported that, following a course of CBT, they initially stopped or reduced their gambling, only to find they relapsed quite quickly because the model, aimed at brief intervention, may not allow enough attention to be paid to the underlying causes of the problem – processing the *reasons* why they are thinking negatively, and so experiencing distressing emotions. These reasons may not lie, or lie only, in current life situations, but in past experience.

By controlling our thoughts and feelings too soon, a valuable opportunity may be missed to listen to the messages that the emotions are giving about what in our life needs to change in order for us to let go of gambling. After all, it is likely that a woman has already been doing just that by gambling – blocking out perceived intolerable emotion, and along with it the need to change what is triggering it. If she is living a life that is inauthentic to her, is it not understandable that she might feel angry and frustrated or depressed? If she suffered childhood trauma, might it not be natural that she feels anxious in intimate relationships? In both cases, it is frequently essential to allow time not only to identify such causes but also to talk them through, so that she can come to terms with the past and change practical here-and-now situations.

I have found many elements of CBT extremely beneficial. It also integrates well with TA, because both models believe that thoughts and feelings influence behaviour.

In a simple and reassuring way, both CBT and TA illustrate to the woman who is confused by her own inner and outer conflicts and contradictions why she is 'addicted' to gambling, despite the fact that there are no drugs or alcohol in her body. If we think of the overview of TA that we have discussed, there are similarities. Both models help people to begin to make sense of things and that is a good place to work from: creating a sound platform of reassuring rationality as a counterbalance to overwhelming emotional intensity and fear.

To identify how a woman's thoughts influence her emotions and behaviour is truly empowering, but it is crucial to do so in a way that does not convey the message that emotions are bad things to have, even the uncomfortable ones. She already feels that, which is why she has been gambling to block them out. Women who have spent much time within mental health services often report, too, that being given more medicalised treatment is a message that their more unsettling thoughts and feelings are signs of illness, and things to be avoided. As a result, they may have a deeper level of fear associated with any emotional experience, because they are afraid of becoming unwell.

A key to becoming and remaining gambling free is identifying perceived intolerable emotion and learning to live with it, to a greater extent than has been possible previously. If we cannot stand and face our fears, we just have to keep on running; keep on gambling. With practice, we can learn to live with most of our emotions to some extent, even though we might never like them, even though they may always be painful or uncomfortable. Often when we begin to accept them, they lose some of their scariness: a bit like a child who, afraid of the dark, always keeps the light on. It's only by sleeping in the dark one night that children learn that, although it might have felt a little scary at first, they survived the experience and will feel a little more comfortable with darkness each time. CBT advocates the skill of 'mindfulness', which encourages learning to observe and sit with thoughts, feelings or addictive urges, instead of distracting oneself from them, or attempting to control them. Ultimately, it may be possible to see that even our most troubling thoughts and emotions pass by eventually.

Keeping a diary to identify thoughts and emotions that trigger gambling can work well for some women. A simple note of key events of the day, along with thoughts and feelings connected to what happened, and a scale of 1–10 for any gambling urges can help to confirm that gambling does not just happen, that it is not an illness, but a reaction: a coping strategy that has gone wrong. Diary keeping can also be a tool to unpick the knotted ball of thoughts, emotions and behaviour, which many women describe as having become like a tangled ball of string. It is helpful to realise that these are separate entities, which have a chain reaction with each other.

For example: *Thought*: I have gambled and so broken the "Be perfect" rule = *Feeling*: shame, guilt and deserving of punishment = *Behaviour*: further gambling to escape feeling.

It is important to judge the appropriateness of diary keeping, or mindfulness, as homework tasks. I have heard reports from some women with a history of child abuse trauma, who have been asked to complete work sheets or diaries of their thoughts and emotions that lead to gambling, and have found this highly distressing. This because their thoughts and feelings were around abuse that they had suffered – sometimes experiencing flashbacks, for example – and to write down details of their thoughts and feelings in an unsupported environment was too distressing. As we have seen in Chapter 6 on assessment, moving into reality is essential, but needs to be at an individual pace because it has usually been avoided with good reason.

For some women, certain emotions do not lose enough of their associated fear ever to be tolerated for very long. Perhaps the Child will always feel scared to some degree in specific situations because of traumatic past experiences. This is where CBT ideas of thought management can be a valuable tool. It can be hugely freeing and empowering to realise that not every negative thought has to be followed through: it is possible to strengthen the rational Adult that can think things through, despite strong emotion, and make healthier decisions. The Child does not have to remain overwhelmed and terrified. There may be a pattern of certain thoughts creating emotions that seem overwhelming, creating a deeper and deeper pit of despair, so that it feels that the only way to climb out for a time is by gambling. If so, it might be time to try looking at healthy distraction tools, or self-soothing exercises: 'A mind too active is no mind at all' (Roethke, 1957).

Women coming into therapy often welcome homework exercises that include coping mechanisms alternative to gambling. I have found that learning to self-soothe, identify enriching life interests, build support networks and, importantly, develop alternative healthy escapisms for times when life just seems too much (or indeed, not enough) are key parts of the therapeutic process. These skills are vital to continued life without gambling, and to discovering an identity and taking a practical place in the world. Working together creatively on how to develop these projects can add a sense of collaboration between the professional and the client. Teamwork increases the engagement in the process. And, of course, engagement with another is all part of reversing the problem gambling cycle, which has been all about disengagement from thoughts, emotions, 'real life' and others in it.

True engagement in the therapeutic relationship is, I have found, the most vital factor in therapy being successful for the woman struggling to change her gambling pattern. As I have emphasised, engagement with the therapist offers greater chance of long-term change, because it is an essential part of reversing the cycle of disengagement, but also, if I might state the obvious, a working relationship must be established for her to want to commit to the work. And no therapeutic work can be done unless she is to commit to being present in the therapy room.

The third model I integrate into my practice is Person-Centred Therapy (PCT) as a way of facilitating a sound working alliance. It is a non-directive approach to a therapeutic working relationship, believing that clients have the potential to make the right choices for themselves, regardless of the therapist's personal values, beliefs and ideas. PCT provides an opportunity to develop a stronger sense of self, and work toward fulfilling one's true potential. A core belief is that we all have the potential to be fully functioning human beings, but that our growth has stunted because of unproductive relational experiences from the moment of birth. The therapeutic relationship aims to provide a sense of a reparative space in which to realise how attitudes, feelings and behaviour are being negatively affected (Rogers, 2000).

I have found that integrating PCT offers a way of being with a client that fosters the kind of therapeutic relationship that will encourage her to stay and work through her gambling problem, and the underlying motivation for it. I realise I have placed PCT last on my list, but it is not to imply it is the least important. In fact, I endeavour to make the following 'core conditions' the cornerstones of my practice:

- Congruence (genuineness);
- Empathy;
- Unconditional positive regard.

To provide an experience of relating with a real person is reassuring and encouraging. When I say a 'real person', I do not believe it often valuable for a professional to disclose personal details, and certainly not every uncensored emerging thought and feeling. Carl Rogers, founder of PCT, himself advocated that personal disclosure should only ever be in the best interest of the client and the therapeutic work. I have found that, as the work progresses and a sound therapeutic relationship is established, many clients find congruence (the sharing of thoughts or emotional experience of what is going on in the therapy room at that moment) encouraging. If I share that I feel sad, for example, in relation to what is happening in that moment, this normalises emotional experiences, which is important after gambling has provided a block to unwanted ones, making emotional intensity feel alien. It is encouraging to have modelled the experiencing and tolerance of an uncomfortable emotion – that it does not have to be destructive, and nothing bad has to happen, as a result of feeling. It challenges the notion that 'Be strong' means 'Don't feel'. Congruence is also about truly relating with another, and so offers practice in relational skills often lost to gambling. It challenges the 'Don't be close' rule.

One women's group meeting was twice disturbed within half an hour by the very nice receptionist at the premises where I held meetings. In her eagerness to pass on a message, she knocked at the door but did not wait for a response before walking into the meeting. I felt genuinely angry about this, and having politely and firmly told the receptionist that this was unacceptable behaviour and I would take her messages later, I chose to share my angry feeling about the incident with the group. I felt this was valuable because many of the women in attendance – like many women who have a gambling problem – had 'Don't feel' and 'Please others' rules playing loudly on their recordings. It was an opportunity to model feeling anger and tolerating it without the predicted 'bad thing' happening, and to point out that it is natural to feel anger at having another cross our boundaries, and that it is okay to establish and protect personal boundaries. Again, this is very valuable, particularly, for women who have a history of abuse or domestic violence.

To repeat one of the messages from this book, the art of congruence – as with most things in life – is all about balance. Congruence can build trust in many women who have had bad experiences with uncertainty, and like to know whom it is they are relating with. They then feel less need to be watchful for nasty surprises, and can engage more fully with the process of becoming gambling free.

I like to know that you are human and that you have feelings, because I thought that normal people don't ever get upset about things. It

> makes me think that maybe there's a chance for me to be a normal person and not panic and gamble, every time I get a problem. (Anonymous group member)

Some women, however, are not ready to hear the feelings of the therapist, imagining that these feelings mean that the therapist will not be strong enough to hold what they need to express, or that they may damage the therapist in some way; or they follow their 'Please others' rule, and look after the therapist. If unspoken, this could be a block to a women opening up and disclosing.

> I'm glad Liz doesn't say anything about her personal life. I think it would be weird. I like coming here because I can say anything and know she'll be okay with it. If I knew about her life I don't think I would feel like that. (Woman in recovery from fruit machine gambling, speaking to a women's group meeting)

Empathy is the ability to see things from the perspective of the woman who is coming along and emptying out the tangled contents of her life, to be unpicked in the therapeutic process. It is the making sense of what might at first seem senseless. What it is *not* is words of sympathy, which are unproductive, and which she will in likelihood distrust and reject, especially early on in therapy when she is often ruthlessly determined to continue to see herself as 'bad'.

Empathy is a practical action. It is demonstrated by actively listening and helping the woman to make sense of how her gambling began, what it was she was attempting to achieve for herself through the behaviour, and what it is that makes it feel so hard to stop. It is the helping her to understand why she has not recognised herself in her actions for so long. It is often the beginning of self-forgiveness for the woman who has bruised herself to the bone with self-recrimination and punishment for what she sees as purely selfish, stupid, meaningless behaviour. Once she can understand what drives her behaviour, and so begin to forgive herself, she can also start to turn down the volume of the critical Parent that only perpetuates the gambling cycle.

I find that using the skills of empathy helps naturally and genuinely to demonstrate the third core condition of unconditional positive regard. As we have discussed, any addiction often leads to desperation, and desperate times lead to desperate measures. It can be difficult to hear the measures that some women have been driven to, as a result of their powerful craving for gambling. It is natural that sometimes professionals might experience uncomfortable thoughts and feelings that conflict with their personal set of values and morals when hearing of, for example, theft, neglect of children and prostitution to get money to gamble, or put food on the table, because all was spent on gambling. Unconditional positive regard is the demonstration of respect towards the woman who is disclosing these issues. This might sound like a tall order. Often I have had clients question whether I am 'just doing my job' in not judging them – that maybe I am playing a role. I am able genuinely to answer that I am not judging, because if I remain interested and curious I am able to understand the *reasons* for their behaviour. If the skill of empathy is both practised and put into practice, the most seemingly illogical behaviour always ends up making sense. Genuine unconditional positive regard facilitates a woman's openness, so providing rich material to work with towards creating a deeper understanding of herself – an understanding, too, of how to develop a good working relationship with her therapist and others, and, most importantly, with all parts of herself. And that, I have found, clears a wide path towards becoming and remaining free of problem gambling.

Carl Rogers described the core conditions as necessary and sufficient for therapeutic growth (Kirschenbaum and Land Henderson, 2001, Chapters 6, 9). I have found that all the models I have described are necessary, but that no one alone is sufficient, which is why I have developed a treatment model integrating elements of all three, working with not just a 'gambler' but a whole woman – helping her to become a more integrated, more resourceful, more aware and enriched self, who needs to gamble to meet her needs less and less; and, wonderfully, to sometimes rediscover the playful, creative Child that has invariably been lost, because gambling and the reasons for gambling scared that part of her away. We cannot play, have fun and be creative if we are afraid.

Chapter 8

Ambivalence

Peter Drucker, influential writer management consultant and social ecologist, spoke of there being a risk one cannot afford to take, and a risk one cannot afford *not* to take (Drucker, 2012). I think this encapsulates the sense of ambivalence around letting go of problem gambling. Which of the risks he describes is a woman's continued gambling? And which risk is stopping gambling? Either could be seen as the woman facing the choice as 'the risk you cannot afford to take'. Both could be viewed as 'the risk you cannot afford *not* to take'. In Chapter 7, we explored how it is perfectly natural for a woman to be in two minds about letting go of problem gambling. We have seen how and why there are different parts of us all that think and feel conflicting things about life choices in general – let alone something that we feel dependent on for psychological and emotional survival:

> A state in which a person concomitantly experiences conflicting feelings, attitudes, drives, desires, or emotions, such as love and hate, tenderness and cruelty, pleasure and pain towards the same person, place, object or situation. To some degree, ambivalence is normal. (American Heritage Medical Dictionary, 2007)

The psychoanalytic theories also consider that a reason for ambivalence is that it often exists because neither option under consideration is likely to be a perfect, clear-cut choice. As we have seen, the woman who gambles *is* involved in a love/hate relationship with gambling. As deeply in dark, obsessional love as she is with gambling, she hates her dependency on it. As much as she loathes her dependency on gambling, she feels enamoured by its transcendent quality, its soothing of her overactive mind and altering of her emotional state.

Ambivalence in itself can be a decidedly uncomfortable feeling, evoking agitation and anxiety as conflicting thoughts and feelings are wrestled with as the 'perfect' choice is searched for. We can work under the misconception that, if it is the right choice, it will both feel absolutely right and make complete logical sense on paper. It is perhaps rarely so, and most choices we make involve an element of sacrifice; to choose one thing, we frequently have to let go of something else. So there is a loss to bear: 'To gain that which is worth having, it may be necessary to lose everything else' (CAIN Web Service, n.d.).

Often procrastination – focusing on other less important matters – can be an avoidance of the discomfort of sitting with ambivalent feelings, as much as ambivalence can be an avoidance of change, loss and other related fears:

> I will stop gambling, I will. I just want to get the house move over and then I will give it everything I've got, I promise you. (Loretta, group member, speaking to the group)

> I won't lie to you, I am going to the casino tonight, but that is the last time I go. I just want to play this one time to see if I can win back some of what I've lost, and then that's me finished with the place. (Carla, one-to-one client, during session)

I use deliberately the term 'letting go' to describe recovery from problem gambling, because it seems to describe the process well and also denote the fact that ultimately a woman has the power to let go – even though it will not initially seem to her as though she had a great deal of choice about it.

Let us recap what it is that she feels is holding on to:

- A means of escape from, and perceived way of coping with, troubling thoughts and emotional pain. If her here-and-now situation is causing her distress, she is buying time out from that, too.
- A sense of predictability and control – although highs and lows, and associated anxiety and depression, are painful, they are familiar, and a paradoxical comfort zone.
- An avoidance of change and associated fears.
- A means of remaining in denial of the destructive consequences of her gambling behaviour. All the time she can keep gambling, she can avoid looking in the mirror at the reality of the high cost of gambling

to excess: not just in financial terms, but in psychological, emotional and physical cost, too, as well as having paid a high price in damaged relationships, jobs and other areas of commitment.

- Hope – hope that gambling one more time might win back some of the money that has been lost and so turn back the clock. Hope that she will not have to face the fact that not only has money been wasted but also her time – the very stuff that our lives are made of. Hope that she might be able to learn to control her gambling behaviour, and so avoid going through what she knows will be a painful withdrawal and grieving for its loss.

Does it not make sense that, given these reasons to keep gambling, any of us would have a little doubt about change? And yet, sadly, sometimes ambivalence can be viewed as a block to beginning therapy. Everyone wanting to come out of the bubble of addiction is ambivalent. There is a vast difference in ambivalence and total resistance to the process of becoming free of problem gambling. Letting go of gambling feels to a woman a high risk. What if she allows herself to go through the process and finds after all she cannot stop? What if the process of therapy leaves her feeling worse? What if she lets go of gambling but finds she cannot cope with how she feels without it when confronted with problems? Some women fear deeply the consequences of not having their tried and tested coping mechanism and have indeed experienced more severely damaging attempts at emotional management, such as self-harm, and used gambling in preference to these. In order to let go, it is encouraging and reassuring, and will make the process more productive, if a woman is aware that she will be offered the chance to exchange gambling for something more rewarding to hold on to.

We have looked at the value of a sound professional relationship, where it is communicated that the person the woman is working with is experienced, resilient and resourceful. Within that relationship, it is possible to use the space to work through ambivalent feelings. It might be useful to determine whether the woman is actually experiencing a high level of ambivalence to the process of change, and not a natural lack of trust in the early stages of therapy. In order to work in the relational and holistic way suggested in this book, the client will need to experience a deep level of trust in the therapist as well as in the therapeutic process, in order to be more fully open and to try out practical strategies to limit gambling. This trust will take some time to grow. I emphasise again (and again) that wherever possible taking time to develop a strong working alliance will be worth every moment invested.

Normalising ambivalence is highly productive. The client may think that she must feel 100 per cent committed to change in order to be accepted for treatment. If she has been fed a diet of too many films and documentaries featuring self-help groups where the message is 'You have to want to do this for yourself', she may keep quiet the fact that actually, at this time, she maybe only wants to do it for her partner or children, or that only half of her wants to do it at all. She may need to hear that that is okay. If there is any part of her at all that wants to 'do this', it is a starting point and something to work with and grow.

Often, I use the image of a set of old-fashioned weighing scales, one half containing the decision to stop gambling, the other containing reasons to continue. Whichever half outweighs the other, they change moment by moment depending on the cost and benefit perceived to be on either side. Entering into a dialogue that will allow the open exploration of what is seen as the value and benefit to the woman of holding onto gambling at a problematic level, weighed up against what may be the value and benefit of letting go of the behaviour, encourages a conscious decision-making process. My experience has been that this needs to be done in a more creative way than merely stating the obvious – that she will not win her money back and gambling is making matters worse. I am happy to take the risk myself of stating here and now that there is not a woman who gambles problematically who really believes in her head or heart that excessive gambling can have a positive outcome, and she will see the professional who tries to tell her so as naive, or at worst not having a clue about what her problem is about, and in all likelihood she will not engage much further in the process.

A more valuable way of helping the woman to weigh up the cost and benefit of her gambling is the use of empathic exploration – as we explored in the last chapter, to go into her world and begin to help her understand how her gambling makes sense to her; to be prepared meta-phorically to roll up sleeves, and go in and get messy, in order to walk out with her into the 'real world'. She will not be dragged out by logical reasoning alone. Chaotic, scary thoughts and emotions got her lost in that world – she did not wake up one morning and make a conscious decision to become a problem gambler because she imagined it made logical sense, or because she did not realise she would lose her money. However irrational the benefit to her of gambling may seem to the outside world, find out why she thinks and feels it makes sense to her on an emotional level, and help her to test out whether the theory that it is helpful to her is true. Stay alongside and express understanding for, and normalise, the reasons why the fears and anxieties she experiences around the change tip her resolve back and forth.

A question I have often found to reap great rewards in terms of information around why it feels hard to commit to letting go of gambling, is to ask how a woman imagines life would feel *without* gambling. The barriers to commitment to becoming gambling free lie less often in logic and more often in fears about how life might be *without* it.

Having stated that a woman will not be dragged out of her tunnel of gambling by logic alone, there is certainly a place for encouraging and modelling a rational thought process. Socratic questioning used alongside empathy helps to test the validity of her beliefs around her gambling experience. The Greek philosopher, Socrates, developed a method of questioning by which we can identify whether our own beliefs or those of others are actually correct. A correct statement, according to Socrates, is one that cannot be rationally contradicted.

Let us take a commonly held belief and statement about problem gambling behaviour, as an example:

Without gambling, my life will be empty.

Socratic method might ask:

Could you ever let go of gambling and have a life more full than it is now?

or

If you keep hold of gambling, does that mean life will always be full?

It is likely that, following this thought process, the woman will begin to see discrepancies in her statement – that perhaps, without so much time and money invested in gambling, she would have more resources to develop a more fulfilling lifestyle. Conversely, that if she keeps hold of gambling, in all likelihood there will never be room in her life for anything – or anyone – else.

This method of exploration encourages the client to work towards her own conclusions and is a way of developing a stronger Adult, which is the part of us that deals with evidence and reality. So begins the building of a greater sense of self-confidence, because it is a step away from being consumed by scary irrational thoughts and feelings from the Child, which can drive the misconception that she cannot stop, cannot manage, without gambling to hide behind.

> 'But a truth supported by reasons and an awareness of counter-arguments was like a statue anchored to the ground by tethering cables.' Socrates' method of thinking promised us a way to develop opinions in which we could, even if confronted with a storm, feel veritable confidence. (de Botton, 2000: 26)

Being anchored in rational thinking can inspire confidence to confront what often feels like the eye of the storm in early recovery:

> What was really good was that you would ask me a question that would make me think and work things out for myself and suddenly the penny would drop. I learnt to question myself and now I almost self-analyse. (Client reflecting on what she found most beneficial about her one-to-one therapy sessions)

An additional and powerful way to develop a person's Adult is to demystify the therapeutic process. As we have discussed, change can be frightening, even if it is that of a positive kind. Past experiences of uncertainty may have negative associations. I have learnt to become comfortable with explaining as far as possible what the process of therapy will entail (detailing frame, boundary and confidentiality policies), and being honest about the fact that there will be some things that neither of us can predict because the client is an individual, but that whatever happens it is a collaborative project with the aim to work through any difficulties.

So very important in working with ambivalence is to help a woman to understand that there are alternative ways of coping that she may discover. Whether they are making changes to her situation, coming to terms with distressing thoughts and feelings, or finding healthier ways of coping and escaping when needed, she will be much more likely to tip the balance in favour of the risk of letting go if she believes there will be something else to hold tightly on to. I have learnt also the value of saying that, 'In my professional experience, yes, women do get through this problem and stop gambling', and to suggest with confidence things that I have witnessed as being of help to other women doing so. The path to freedom from problem gambling can be a lonely one. It inspires confidence in the woman taking the risk of the first steps if her sense is that the person she is working with has walked with others that way before.

If ambivalence is intensifying during the work, it might be worth checking whether any homework to encourage coping without gambling is proving a little too difficult. Let us remember many women come along obeying the 'Please others' Rule and at first may treat the professional no differently. If a sudden drop in attendance at appointments begins, it might be an indication that a woman is afraid to reveal that she is failing to manage to reduce gambling, and is afraid of the therapist's reaction or confronting her own feelings of shame or embarrassment at not managing or not attempting tasks. If so, lowering expectations of any goal-focused work might be necessary.

One long-term client of both one-to-one and group work drew an image representing her ambivalence. She drew a desert island on which there was one palm tree producing coconuts and a stream for water. Otherwise the island was barren. Just on the horizon was another island, lush with vegetation and inhabited by friendly people, whom she felt would welcome her. To get to the other island, she would have to cross deep, turbulent seas. All she had available to make the crossing was a raft, with oars. She said that what made the difference to her having the courage to set sail into the uncharted waters, to cross to the unknown island, was knowing that she would have me as her therapist and support from the women's group, when it got stormy, or if she were to lose direction, or be too tired to row for a while.

A woman may need to attach and hold on tightly to the therapeutic relationship as she makes the transition from attachment to her gambling problem and re-attachment to the 'real' world and relationships within it. The therapist and therapeutic process fulfil the role of a halfway house.

Of course, all appropriate therapeutic boundaries should be maintained at all times and the relationship between therapist and client kept within the container of the consulting room. Within that space, however, real depth of engagement in a trusted working relationship will certainly tip the balance in favour of taking the risk of life without problematic gambling. We shall talk about the absolute treasure trove of personal growth, reassurance, connectedness and joy at the realisation that is gained from understanding one does not have to be alone, when we touch on the experience of women-only gambling therapy groups later on.

A model encompassing the key points we have discussed in this chapter is offered by Motivational Interviewing (MI) developed by William R Miller in 1983 as a result of his experience of working in the field of alcohol treatment. It is now an established evidence-based practice used in substance misuse and problem gambling treatment, for the encouragement and motivation for change. It does not impose change and this is important, given the need of the majority of women who have a gambling problem to feel in control, and who feel uncomfortable with the idea of another having power over them. It does support and facilitate change at a pace and structure that is tailor-made to the individual.

MI invites a client to have a conversation about change as a possibility, and so can include Socratic-style questioning. It has an emphasis on a collaborative way of working, so again lessening the likelihood of the client experiencing a potentially threatening imbalance of power, while increasing opportunities for her to grow her Adult. The focus is on bringing out her own motivation and commitment to the process of change and letting go. As Socrates believed, she is much more likely to feel 'anchored to the ground' if supported by reasons and counterarguments that are self-generated. She will then both think and feel that it makes sense to commit to change, even if she still experiences a little ambivalence at times.

There are four principles of MI:

1.   Expressing empathy;
2.   Developing a discrepancy;
3.   Rolling with resistance;
4.   Developing self-efficacy.

Regarding empathy, it is hoped that by now readers have an understanding of why I stress the value and importance of empathy.

Developing a discrepancy – exploring a woman's beliefs about how her gambling is working positively for her, and how she imagines life would be without it. Then using Socratic questioning to do detective work together, to discover if there are discrepancies in her theory.

Andrea's story is an example.

Andrea

Andrea believed that her online gambling helped to ease her anxieties around her stressful job. Without gambling, she imagined her anxieties would spiral out of control and she would break down and end up having to leave her job. We explored that for the time she was gambling she found the experience soothing. When she stopped, however, it would often be at around 2 a.m., by which time she would get a maximum of four hours' sleep. She would not have eaten during that period because her focus was totally on the gambling experience. If she had spent all her money, she would have to walk to work that day, instead of taking a bus. She would arrive exhausted, feeling weak, vulnerable and already anxious, and therefore less able to cope with the stress of work than if she had not gambled.

For Andrea, rationally understanding that her theory about the function gambling served for her did not hold water, did not in itself make her stop, but it was enough to tip the balance of ambivalence to deciding to commit to the process of stopping.

Developing self-efficacy – encouraging stronger coping skills and a view of oneself as a capable, more independent being. For Andrea, realising that she was not going to be asked to let go of gambling and have nothing else to hold on to was also the encouragement she needed. We discussed how it was possible to learn to manage not only her high anxiety levels in healthier ways, such as better eating and sleeping patterns, but that changes at work might be possible if she approached HR or asked her manager to adjust her hours.

Rolling with resistance – if we take resistance to mean ambivalence, the idea of 'rolling with' it instead of pushing against it surely makes sense. If we take as a given that a woman's gambling is a form of defence, she is likely to hold onto it even more tightly if she feels it is being dragged out of her grasp. A professional who is too challenging, too soon, and views – or at worst verbalises – ambivalence as a resistance to the process and an 'excuse' to keep gambling may be seen as attacking. If we feel attacked, do we not attack back, or defend more strongly? Or run and hide to protect what we feel is under attack and we are in danger of losing? The end result of too strong and mistimed a challenge to ambivalence or resistance can be a breakdown in the working relationship, with a pretence from the client that she wholeheartedly wants to stop gambling, to please the professional, yet going underground with her ambivalence. It is much better to go with the ebb and flow of her commitment, which may alter week to week. One good week gambling free can fill her with confidence to carry on. The following week, one emotionally distressing event, missing her coping mechanism, and possibly a relapse to gambling behaviour can make her question her capacity to continue with the recovery process.

This chapter is towards understanding that ambivalence is not the same as resistance – it is a defence mechanism we all employ to varying degrees and at various times, out of fear of making the wrong decision, and because decisions are rarely neatly packaged in boxes marked the 'right' one or the 'wrong' one, and so provoke anxiety and involve *risk*. As contradictory as it may seem, readers will understand by this stage that risk is something the woman who gambles is rarely comfortable with taking.

Chapter 9

Understanding why

It is clear that problem gambling for the majority of woman is a means of escape from psychological distress and emotional pain. It is an attempt to manage what feels unmanageable. In order for treatment to be effective, and especially to prevent relapse and cross-addiction, it is crucial to identify what it is that is causing such pain before one can work to make changes in that area.

In the tight grip of addiction, fear is always a presence and problem gambling in no exception to that rule. The underlying motivation for gambling behaviour is often fear based, and fear is then intensified by the consequences of the behaviour. As we have explored in Chapter 8, fear is also attached to letting go of problem gambling. If anything, with gambling, fear is more intensely present than it might be with any other form of addiction. Drugs or alcohol remain in the system after the actual act of ingestion and can take the edge off life for longer, with the coming down often more gradual. With problem gambling, the narcotic effect lasts only as long as physical engagement with the gambling activity. And that can last only as long as the money does. The 'come down' could more accurately described as a 'crash down', with the impact triggering instant awareness of the damage that has been done. The emotional and psychological impacts are similar with any addiction. However, what do remain in a more damaging way than with any other addiction, are the often long-term financial consequences, resulting from having begged, stolen or borrowed the limitless amounts of money needed to feed a gambling addiction. Both men and women I have treated who have previously battled drug and alcohol problems, when sickened and reeling from the financial impact of problem gambling have spoken of there being always a physical limit to how much one can drink, or how many drugs one can take. A limit, therefore, to how much money can be lost. With gambling, however, there are no physical limitations. The only limits are set by the amount of money that can be accessed, the limits often pushed until there is no more money left to 'drown sorrows' or 'buy a high through gambling': 'I've taken every drug there is and got over it, but thinking of the thousands I've lost to gambling, it's killing me. It's destroyed my life' (male online gambler, 28 years old).

These anxieties in themselves can then become a distraction from 'real life'. Worrying about how to get out of another financial crisis can be a way to avoid facing and dealing with real-life issues – the issues that drive the gambling behaviour. This level of fear causes confusion and can lead to depression, making healthy decisions difficult and escape from the trap of pathological gambling feel impossible. Fear freezes.

The 'fight', 'flight', or 'freeze' response to fear and times of acute stress was first described by Walter Bradford Cannon (1871–1945), an American physiologist professor at Harvard University (Bradford Cannon, 1915). Animals react to threats with an instant activation of the sympathetic nervous system. Adrenalin is secreted in preparation for rapid response – within seconds – to the perceived threat. The animal will then fight to defend itself, run away to avoid attack, or 'play dead' until the danger passes.

We, the human animal, are biologically equipped with the same response mechanism to take instantaneous action to protect ourselves and to survive situations of acute stress and danger. And yet how hard we have worked to condition ourselves to respond in ways that go against our instinctual nature. We keep ourselves in traps that any other animal would fight to get free of, we remain in jobs, relationships, life situations that bring us little happiness and fulfilment and that any other animal would take flight from. We push ourselves forward into increasingly stressful situations, increase our debt, take on second jobs, and more and more responsibility, where animals would freeze and say an inward 'enough of this, to keep going along this path makes no sense'. I had a conversation with two friends recently; we had all found that on the previous bitterly cold, windy, rainy day our dogs had refused to go for a walk and had literally frozen on the pavement, determinedly sitting down and refusing to put themselves through the uncomfortable experience just to please their owners, who had thought it made logical sense that their dogs should walk. Who was the more sensible, in the literal meaning of the word . . . ?

Clarissa Pinkola Estés, Jungian analyst, wrote the well-known book on feminine psychology, *Women Who Run With the Wolves*, following her study of wildlife biology and, in particular, wolves:

> Healthy wolves and healthy women share certain psychic charac-
> teristics; keen sensing, playful spirit, and a heightened capacity for
> devotion. Wolves and women are relational by nature, inquiring,
> possessed of great endurance and strength. They are deeply intuitive,
> intensely concerned with their young, their mates and their pack.
> They are experienced in adapting to constantly changing circum-
> stances; they are fiercely stalwart and brave. (Estés, 1992: 2)

Excessive gambling is an attempt to follow through on the flight
instinct. In humans, flight can manifest as withdrawal *from relationship*
and being drawn *to addiction*. As we have discussed, these movements
are intrinsically linked in the area of women and problem gambling. In
running to addiction, a woman loses touch with what Estés describes in
the extract as the instinctual nature of woman as she numbs her senses
and cuts herself off from relational experience. A reason I believe that
gambling often appears to be even more deeply destructive to women than
to men is that the core strengths of what it is to be a woman, which Estés
identifies, have been weakened to the point of collapse.

So, if fear underlies a woman's gambling, how does she identify
exactly what the triggers – situational, psychological and emotional – are?
What is it that she is so afraid of? I have found that the way to discover
triggers is in the situation that experience has shown me is the *primary*
trigger for problem gambling, and that is in relationship.

We have looked at the essential ingredients of the one-to-one
therapeutic relationship and the benefits that these will bring in terms of
engagement with the process of therapy, and the time and space this
provides to work through the recovery process. A richly rewarding part
of this process is in examining and learning from what arises in the
relationship between the professional and the client. If the clinical setting
allows time for attention to be paid to the developing working relationship, sooner or later ways in which the client relates to others in the
world outside will be seen in the relationship between her and the
therapist. The therapeutic relationship, in the sense that I describe it in
this book, is a psychologically and emotionally intimate relationship in
which the woman is invited to connect and gradually reveal her uncensored self to another. All her fears regarding past experiences of close
relationships with others will transpire eventually in the consulting room,
along with the ways she has avoided the fearful feelings and/or re-
experiencing the situations that brought the fears of relating into being.

Louise's story offers an example.

Louise

Louise lived her life by a 'Please others' rule. She was invariably compliant in our sessions and responded to my telling her I was taking two weeks' holiday by saying she was fine and understood that I was human and needed a break. In actuality, Louise was angry and upset that I would be unavailable. She had frozen her true feelings because her fear was that I would reject and abandon her if she told me how she felt. As a child, she had never felt secure with her mother who was frequently absent and so she had learnt to please her mother in the hope that she would want to spend more time at home. She had transferred her experiences of her mother onto me, and her experiences of their relationship on to ours. The result of her not fighting for her time and space by expressing her true feelings to me was that she gambled to take flight from them. Exploring this dynamic together helped Louise to identify her 'Please others' rule and her fear of rejection, which she had used the rule to protect herself from. She understood that it had led her to a lifestyle that was all about caring for others and putting their needs first, but that it was okay to demonstrate enough to stand up for her own wants and needs.

What we see in Louise's example is how her problems in being her authentic self in close relationships originated in her family. Our family relationships are our first experience of what it is to be in a group situation and therefore inform our expectations of how all our future experiences of group involvement will be: from school to the workplace. I have discovered that working in a therapeutic group setting is potentially a transformational experience for women who gamble problematically. It is also the most feared, because it was in the family group that the woman learnt her rules for life and ways of relating that have led to the point at which she is at now. Coming into a group, she will transfer all her anxieties around relationship, not just onto one person but onto all others in the group.

This is profoundly challenging and most women have a high level of ambivalence at first around committing to group therapy. Having spent a good portion of their lives avoiding relationship difficulties and the associated fear and pain, 'Don't be close' is a rule they live by. They are reluctant to deliberately put themselves into the arena of relationship again. Even if they are not consciously aware that their gambling has been triggered by relationship issues, they know that they feel uncomfortable around others.

The reasons women fear a group setting, however, are the reasons that group therapy works so well. It is a microcosm of a woman's relational world, as is one-to-one therapy, but it offers potential for even greater self-understanding as she relates within a broader spectrum of personalities and more challenging situations. Experience has taught me the value of offering open, and open-ended groups. The art of living requires that we are able to manage uncertainty, including developing new attachments and dealing with loss. The groups I facilitate allow new members to come, and others to go, at various periods of the process of that group, thus replicating as far as possible how life and relationship are on the outside. These experiences offer insight and understanding for group members as to how these issues have an impact on them and influence their gambling behaviour. They also offer a safe space in which to practise new and healthier ways of relating.

Group members are standing and confronting their fears instead of taking flight from them. We have explored the fears a woman brings along with her to one-to-one therapy, so let us imagine these fears multiplied by the number of other group members – potentially times ten. Despite her fears, she may have been fairly certain of a professional, non-judgemental response from her one-to-one therapist, but here is a group of her peers. There are so many variables as to how they might respond to her disclosures. They may even see through her non-disclosures: they know what it is to gamble, to conceal, to deny and to tell lies, and she fears instant transparency. It may be harder than in the world outside to hide, or to pretend that all is okay.

The woman fears similarities to others in a group because it will be less easy to hide and she will risk her real self being exposed. She fears hearing similarities in the stories of others, too, because she will hear, and see reflected back, aspects of herself of which she has been in denial. She fears difference too. What if the others are free of gambling and she is still battling with cravings and relapse? What if the others are still gambling when she is gambling free? These fears represent how it feels to belong to any social group and to fear the consequences of not *really* belonging: of being the odd one out. If she takes the risk of allowing herself to belong, and to be herself, she takes the risk of rejection and exclusion.

I have noted that the only occasions when group members have wished to exclude another member is when they perceive her to be actively lying to conceal her true self. There seems to have been an instinctual knowing in the collective group on the rare occasion that this has happened. The other group members will pull closer together at these times, as a protection strategy. And they have sometimes confronted the member they do not trust. We see fear of uncertainty and the unknown, associated with a negative outcome, in action in the group at these times.

A woman may experience all these fears of meeting and connecting with other women in the here and now, plus carrying in a metaphorical bag full of old fears and experiences of intimacy with other women to transfer to the others she will meet in a group. Many women who have attended a group have disclosed stories of betrayal by other significant women in their life. I have noted how such betrayals often seem to have a deeper impact than negative treatment they have received from key male figures in their life, and even more so if there has been a difficult relationship between a woman and her mother. If distant from her mother, a woman may have not had the opportunity to learn from her how to be a woman in the world. This lack of closeness with her mother, or other key female caregivers, might have left her feeling excluded from her same-sex group, and created a 'Don't belong' rule. Her mother's own relationship with the outside world will have influenced her own concept of it. If her mother experienced the world as dangerous, and was over-protective, she may have been living with a 'Don't grow up' rule, and have a naïve and fearful view of relationships and engagement with the world in general. A difficulty in forming healthily close bonds with other women correlates with a lack of the emotional support that these relationships can bring:

> Yet both the historical and psychological research on women's friendship indicates that, far from being trivial and fickle, such friendships tend to be deep, intimate and enduring . . . These relationships have emphasised self-disclosure, emotional closeness, and empathy, and have been a core part of women's emotional lives. (Lips, 2006: 210)

With the exception of a framework and boundaries, and being guided by the therapeutic models I described earlier in this book, a women's group is organic. It *is* the members in it at any given time. In order for anything at all to happen, there has to be a level of interaction and engagement. The women who attend take on responsibility for growing a group, through continuing their growing relationship with themselves and with others within the group. As the relationships form and deepen in the group, women find themselves falling into old, stuck relational patterns with other members. They also find themselves falling back onto old survival skills that in all likelihood they learnt as a child in their original family group. The rules they have lived their lives by are clearly seen as they attempt to 'Please others' or 'Be strong', and hold authentic thoughts and feelings tightly inside in order to obey 'Don't be close' or 'Don't belong'. With 84 per cent of group members over the last six years presenting with histories of child abuse or domestic violence, the adherence to the rules may be especially prevalent because the abuse they have experienced still has a strong impact strongly on their worldview:

> The assault is not (or not only) upon the physical body but upon . . . the individual's perception of the self as valuable . . . the individual's perception of the self as competent . . . (and, among other things) the individual's perception that the world is beneficent or neutral rather than innately hostile. (Brierre, 1992: 24)

Beck and Emery's (1985) cognitive model of anxiety disorder and abuse-related anxiety described the following symptoms:

- Hypervigilance to danger in the environment, whether objectively warranted or not.
- Preoccupation with control, with the belief that even a slight loss of self-determination or self-protection could lead to danger or catastrophe.
- Misinterpretation of objectively neutral or positive interpersonal stimuli as evidence of threat or danger.

The above view of world and relationship has often triggered problem gambling behaviour because it has kept a woman at distance from potentially supportive relationship, and so from avenues of emotional expression. The suppression of excessive gambling has taken the place of close relationship. Gambling seems to offer the unconditional relationship that will always welcome her with open arms. Her hypervigilance will have made her ever-watchful for danger, and she is likely to have developed a highly sensitive 'filtration system' that she will use to discard anything positive offered by interpersonal relationship, because it will not be trusted; yet she will focus on what she feels may contain signs of danger. Living with such a high level of background anxiety for long periods may have resulted in panic attacks, which is the result of her interpreting bodily responses to acute stress (i.e. rapid heart rate, sweating, hyperventilation resulting in feeling faint) as signs of critical illness, such as heart attack or stroke. If this reaction has been triggered by situations of close contact with others, she may have avoided such situations in an attempt to manage her panic attacks. Gambling has often been a distraction technique aimed at stopping the cycle of panic. To see old behaviour patterns activated and reflected to her in a group provides a new and in many ways unique opportunity. She can formulate a personal agenda for her group meetings that goes beyond stopping the problematic gambling behaviour, and use the group as a mirror in which to see how her beliefs and behaviours affect her behaviour and relational patterns.

Hilary's story offers an example:

Hilary

Hilary was a survivor of child abuse. Her mother had warned her that, if she told anyone, it would only get worse and that nobody would believe her anyway. For the large part of her 45 years, apart from in her workplace, Hilary had remained largely isolated. After nine months of one-to-one therapy, she found the courage to come into a group. Despite having by that stage formed a strong working alliance with me in one-to-one therapy, in the group she once again reverted to 'Don't be close' in an attempt to tolerate the high anxiety she felt at being in close proximity to others. She began to freeze with fear, sitting in silence for most of the sessions apart from checking in, and checking out, when she would be brief and factual. She became highly critical of me as the facilitator. We later identified that this was because in the group she transferred her thoughts and feelings about her mother onto me. The group reminded her of her family group, and I as the authority figure represented her mother. The value for Hilary in recognising this was that she could agree her own personal agenda within the group and practise finding her own voice in order to express formerly suppressed thoughts and feelings and to learn that 'fight' in the form of assertiveness was a positive thing.

The suppression of the fight instinct is a common trigger for problem gambling in women. Again and again it is seen in a group that a woman who attends her first few meetings follows 'Please others', 'Be perfect',

'Don't be important' rules, which throughout life precluded her from expressing anger. She grew up believing that little girls should be made of 'sugar and spice and all things nice'. Perhaps she witnessed anger used destructively and fears something bad will happen if she contacts her angry feelings. Gambling has helped her to push them back down when they have begun to surface. In the group, developing closeness with others may provoke them and the perceived threats attached to this. Perhaps another group member reminds her of past characters in her life that she has felt anger towards. Without gambling to hide it, it will be harder for her to escape her anger. When it does surface in the group, it may be in the form of intense expression. Anger is a strong energy that urges us to action, and years of inaction have only added fuel to the fire. Expression of anger is often followed quickly by fears of negative judgement from other group members: fear of rejection or even attack. If any conflict does arise in a group, it is dealt with by identifying what it is that the woman feels angry about, working out if it has any connections with her past experiences and looking towards the future – how she can maintain a healthy and appropriate level of expression of anger, thus lessening the need to suppress it with further gambling.

Gambling, too, can at times be a silent expression of anger. One woman who lived life by 'Please others' was secretly raging at her partner for pushing her to declare bankruptcy. For her this was the ultimate shame. She did not verbalise the strength of her anger, because she had many negative experiences of witnessing anger expressed aggressively in childhood. Her immediate relapse involving the gambling of all monies from the sale of the family home in two days, was her screaming her anger through her behaviour.

I have spoken of so many women being afraid of the power of their own anger, but many women are fearful of the powerlessness they feel with they experience sadness. A women who has lived with the 'Be strong' rule may feel ashamed of being tearful, seeing it as a sign of weakness. Going back to fight, flight or freeze – the basic animal responses to threat – what happens to an animal if it is vulnerable? It is open to attack and destruction by others. This is a sense of what a woman fears from the world outside of a group and it will present inside the group, manifesting perhaps as freezing; she may sit silently and avoid engagement with others to lessen the impact of their stories upon her. Her gambling has been an attempt to remain strong by freezing, keeping herself in the stasis of addiction where oddly all is predictable and there is little chance of scary changes. She may use 'fight' to mask her feelings of upset by becoming angry if others get close to her softer emotions, or by presenting herself physically as unfeminine, a 'tough cookie'. During the process of the group, it is likely that others will see through the suit of armour she is wearing and hold up a metaphorical mirror, reflecting to her what they see. If she can begin to allow herself emotional expression and see that her tears can lead to relief, and to her needs for support being met, she may feel a sense of relief she has never experienced through gambling, which has only left her more sad, weak and vulnerable. She can learn that being truly strong has a new and deeper meaning, as it is translated from harshness, aggression and suppression into the ability to sit with pain.

I often speak in a group of it being a space in which to learn how to take off masks worn for the outside world. Self-disclosure must take place if group therapy is to be successful. It is important to note, however, that it must never be forced and is of little use if it is, because it will result in breakdown of trust, non-attendance, or merely the telling of a story, yet without feeling attached to it, because feeling may still be numbed as a protective factor against becoming overwhelmed. Self-disclosure is important not just as a means of gaining more material for self-exploration, but as an opportunity to discover how it *feels* to self-disclose, to engage and to be seen by others, bearing in mind problem gambling is all about achieving the opposite effect. What is it about that level of intimacy a woman avoids? What does she believe are the implications for relationship?

The clarity with which group members see each other through their shared experiences is an invaluable tool for identifying triggers for problem gambling and indeed other addictions that have preceded it, or run alongside it. Yes, group members recognise traits of problem gambling behaviour; but equally important is that they more often than not recognise the underlying life and relationship issues that led to it. Abandonment, abuse, betrayal and rejection are recurring themes of stories shared in a group. These resonate with members, as they listen to the telling, and shed light and understanding on the *reasons* for their own behaviour, which they may have termed merely 'excuses', feeling until then too deep a level of guilt and shame to allow any degree of compassion and forgiveness towards themselves. And yet, as they invariably experience these feelings for another, as they hear of that person's life journey and the traps she has fallen into along the way, they reflect on the fact that there is a difference between reasons and excuses, and that for themselves the only difference was feeling they had not deserved self–understanding; and, of course, they come to understand that there is a difference in taking responsibility for the self and behaviour, and self-recrimination, which only serves as a trigger to further gambling.

Sometimes in a group, on hearing another's painful and troubling story, we will see patterns of avoidance of pain in action. A group member who has felt a victim in her own life will often make rescue attempts on hearing or seeing the distress of another group member. Rescue attempts may involve offering her fellow group member a positive interpretation of what she has just shared with the group, changing the topic of conversation, or using humour to 'airlift' the group out of the depths of emotion. What we are seeing in action is in all likelihood a time she would be tempted to gamble if outside the group, because she is attempting to take flight from perceived intolerable emotion. One woman described seeing before her eyes the slot machine game she had been playing the previous evening, when the topic discussed resonated with the deep level of sadness and guilt she felt – a sign that this was what she was escaping from through gambling when outside the group, and thereby identifying a valuable area for her to work through.

On occasion in a group I have witnessed attempts at, or threats of, physical flight from uncomfortable emotion representative of times when a woman would run to gamble if outside group. Women who are deeply afraid of sitting with – having witnessed – specific emotions also may also attempt to drown out their feelings by drinking more water than usual, or breaking the spell of the intensity of the group circle by absenting themselves to use the bathroom, or stating their intention to leave the group altogether because they cannot stand feeling upset and/or angry. Again, these moments contain precious nuggets in their pain and discomfort, because a woman has a chance to reflect on what it is she is running from; why she fears it so terribly; and what triggered the association of pain and fear with that emotion. If only she can bring herself to stay – which I always strongly encourage – she has an opportunity to begin to sit with, and work through, her own pain. Finally, she can stop running. This is not only a way to identify the triggers for her gambling problem, but also an essential skill to develop for prevention of relapse, which we will now explore in Chapter 10.

Chapter 10

Relapse prevention

We have now travelled far along the path of problem gambling – from taking the first steps identifying reasons for a woman's problem gambling behaviour and her becoming lost in the fog of addiction, to her summoning the courage to make changes, and exploring the value of professional support as a guide for that journey. So, let us stand here with the woman who has been along that path, so far that she is now free of problem gambling behaviour. Surely, that is the end point, and a time to place a flag in the ground to mark the end of a successful adventure? To answer that question, let us see what it is that she might now be looking out at, bearing in mind that gambling to the extent that she has been will have occupied so much territory in her life. Not only will she have spent a great deal of her time physically engaged in the activity, but when not in the act of gambling she will have been preoccupied with the negative consequences of her last gamble, or planning how she might gamble again, or battling with urges to do so. So, viewed from her perspective, the landscape of her life without gambling can appear barren, bleak, uninspiring and maybe more than a little scary too. Despite the pain and chaos of gambling, she knew the territory well. There are now large areas of emptiness and unfamiliar ground stretching ahead of her, and that leaves her open to new experience, new people, new self-discoveries, all of which can be wonderfully exciting, but conversely anxiety-provoking too. Let us remember that one of her reasons for choosing gambling as a coping mechanism was that she wanted to feel in control.

The woman who gambles excessively has layer upon layer of suppression strategies, from the 'Rules' for life by which she has lived, to addiction or self-harming behaviour. All have been attempts to silence her inner voice, so that she does not hear for herself how miserable life has become, and/or so that others do not hear her speak the truth that she fears they will in some way judge and punish her for. Before she can begin to draw a new life map, she needs to begin to develop a greater sense of identity, to learn what it is she likes and dislikes, what she wants, needs and enjoys, and to find ways of expressing herself not only verbally, but also through her re-engagement with life in all key areas from relationships, work, recreational activities through to art and spirituality. After all, would it not make sense for her to be tempted to turn around and head back the way she has just come if she does not know where she is going? Or if the dangers she perceived to be lurking around the corner are still there, and all she has done is cut off her means of escape?

> One of the greatest difficulties in dealing with food addicts, as with alcoholics, is helping them to overcome their sense of despair when they lose the high associated with those addictions. (Woodman, 1982: 27)

Jungian analyst Marion Woodman's words are no less true for the woman missing the escapism, the transcendent quality, of gambling. The depression she initially experiences without it is a dark, grey void. Life feels empty and meaningless. She lacks energy and motivation to make positive changes and there is high risk of relapse as she battles with craving something, almost anything, to lift her mood.

Relapse is often described as 'I was straight back in there, and if anything even worse than before!' If gambling ever was, for the woman concerned, a gradual slide along the spectrum to problem or pathological gambling, relapse – especially in early recovery – often has none of the gradual escalation. An element of this is I believe the shock and disappointment of the relapse, creating such anxiety and frustration that these increase the sense of urgency to stay and escape from the feelings the slip itself generated. An additional reason seems to be that in relapse there is a heightened sense of relief in re-engaging in the grieved-for escapism, and so the desperation to cling onto time-out from painful withdrawal, and what feels like an all too 'real' world.

Relapse is often acutely painful and distressing, but also valuable. Not only is it an opportunity to learn more about what triggers gambling, but the sharp 'in the moment' comparison with a life gambling free, and a life of problem gambling, can be further relapse prevention in itself. This is especially the case for the woman who is far enough in recovery to have been beyond the pit of despair of early gambling-free withdrawal, to have experienced a sense of relief, calm and empowerment without the chaos and preoccupation problem gambling brings. To re-experience the heightened anxiety and roller coaster of emotions and racing, chaotic thoughts, can re-enforce her decision that she is better off gambling free, that gambling is not worth the price of pain and disruption to her psychological and emotional world. Having said this, repeated relapse after building the foundations of a new life can leave her feeling disheartened and disappointed. One way in which she may begin to protect herself against further disappointment is by freezing the creation of her productive new life; what is the point of going to the effort of making a better life for herself if regular relapses are going to destroy her efforts? This stuckness only perpetuates the likelihood of further relapse as she sits in limbo – no longer in the world of gambling, but neither fully engaged in life beyond it. She may also feel anger with herself for relapsing: 'What part of me was *so stupid* I didn't realise I would pay *this* price of pain if I went back (to gamble) . . . ?' (woman, 45 years old, one day after relapse).

The woman's anger with herself may prevent her from revealing her relapse because she feels she is unworthy of the support she needs at this time. Relapse can also be dragged underground by embarrassment and shame. The woman may feel she has used up all her chances with family and friends who have been supportive and patient; that her relapse will be seen as ingratitude for all they have done for her. If she is in professional support, despite it being emphasised that relapse is natural in the process, she may feel similarly. Many clients, on disclosure of relapse, have apologised for 'wasting my time' and 'letting me down'. If she is, as so many women I work with, more used to caring for others than herself, this also represents the difficulties she has in accepting care. The barriers to relationship may be drawn back up because, anticipating rejection from others, she may reject them first.

In order to prevent relapse, the following practical strategies may be useful:

- Self-exclude oneself from the chosen gambling venue;
- Download software to block access gambling sites on computers;
- Block access to gambling sites on mobile phones or interactive television;
- Hand control of finances to a trusted other;
- Arrange limited access to cash and bank cards;
- Spend time in alternative pleasant activities.

Although helpful, none of these strategies is a panacea. In early recovery from problem gambling, one of the areas of greatest difficulty is in dealing with the void a woman faces. She has lost the absorption of gambling *and* the routine and ritual that it gave her every day or week: 'Every week I'd tell myself I wasn't going to do it (gamble), that I will buy myself something nice instead, but I never did. But even telling myself that became a pattern. Same thing every Wednesday' (woman in second session of one-to-one therapy).

If we think about our routines, they are automatic processes: we do not have to be present or conscious in that moment because we repeat the activity each and every day. This is why we make our cups of tea in the morning, or arrive by our regular train to work, and do not remember a thing about it. We can remain detached. If our routine gets disturbed, *how* disturbed are we! Suddenly, we have to be present, to think consciously; we feel unsettled and irritable without our tea before work, or we have to work out alternative routes when our train is cancelled.

On a grander scale for a woman in early gambling recovery, the removal from her life of the routine and ritual provided by her gambling habit will leave her too often painfully present and more conscious of a life she has been seeking detachment from, and leave a vacuum experienced as an aching emptiness as she misses and grieves the loss of gambling.

In the early days and weeks, the grieving process and accompanying anxiety and sadness around the loss will be to the forefront of the woman's mind as she battles with inner conflicts and cravings. To prevent relapse, it is vital that she has space to express these feelings of loss and despair, and that she is offered support and reassurance that these are normal. This is frequently best offered in a professional space, as even the most supportive and understanding of partners, family and friends may be frightened and frustrated at hearing the woman speak of how the loss of gambling is having an impact on her, and may interpret this as a wish or intention to return to the behaviour. If she does not express and work through these feelings, she is only too experienced with the alternative – suppressing them through gambling.

At this time it will be reassuring for the woman to build a new routine, new rituals that give a sound framework to life while she feels internally in chaos. Routine and ritual bring a sense of continuity to life, a sense that life continues without gambling, and they stop her being frozen to the spot by fear of living without it. New routines may begin with just the basics, such as getting up at a regular time each day, developing healthy eating patterns, paying bills, meeting established commitments and honouring new ones too, such as attending appointments for therapeutic support. With repetition, the woman's new routine will be established as an automatic process and can bring welcome relief to her overworked, overanxious mind, as well as helping her to begin to grow a sense of self-efficacy. After patterns of living a life of continually letting herself and others down, she sees it is possible for her to depend on herself to get things done. With good foundations firmly in place, she will have more conscious attention free to focus on moving forward beyond life lived at a basic survival level.

In these early days of recovery, keeping as busy as possible helps to avoid giving into cravings because she will find that, if she follows through on a gambling-related thought, it will quickly lead to urges to gamble.

As the woman begins to settle more into life without gambling, her thoughts will develop greater clarity, and awareness of the underlying reasons for her gambling will start to surface. This is potentially another dangerous time in terms of relapse, as her thoughts and the uncomfortable feelings they trigger once again create urges to gamble.

Whatever the trigger in terms of external factors, whether it be from childhood or a difficult current life situation, whether it is connected to trauma of a physical, sexual or psychological nature, ultimately it is the *emotional* impact of it that the woman will have been escaping from. Therefore, if by this stage she is beginning to be clearly aware of which *feeling* is intolerable – the emotional trigger for gambling – she will more easily find what it is that she needs to cope with that *specific* feeling, and so better deal with cravings when they arise.

In my therapeutic work, I encourage curiosity about a woman's gambling and her asking herself the question, 'What did I *really* need the last time I gambled?' The answer will vary individual to individual, but is often along the themes of:

> I needed emotional warmth.
> I needed to feel secure.
> I needed a hug.
> I needed somebody to talk to.

Matching a new coping strategy that fits with the *true need* that was hidden behind the need for gambling, the woman will experience a difference in that she is capable of meeting her emotional needs rather than concealing and exacerbating them, as she was when gambling.

Learning techniques that help to prevent the build-up of anger, such as assertiveness, are helpful because the woman will develop skills for dealing with incidents as they arise, instead of waiting until each anger-provoking incident builds to an explosive level, whereby she will be tempted to gamble to push down the feared volcanic explosion. It is helpful for her to learn to discern the various types of anger she experiences, and that sometimes it may be valuable to let a raging anger that wants to present in a physical form do just so – beat a pillow, scream into a pillow. Better the pillow gets it than the woman ends up beating herself up, or screaming silently inside.

Sadness or 'upset' feelings often need to be soothed and comforted. When feeling vulnerable, many women have found that taking a warm relaxing bath, or spending an evening under the duvet in front of a favourite film might be all that is needed to take the edge off of gambling urges. Simple, and yet effective, this is a part of a woman just giving herself permission *to feel what it is she feels*, without thinking she has to hurry herself away from it. In a world where we are flooded with messages that pain – physical or emotional – is something to fear and avoid, to accept it as a normal and natural part of the human condition that will come and go can be reassuring and soothing in itself.

Some women, after many years' gambling, or with associated trauma, may have lost touch with what it is they feel As one woman told me on her first session, 'I don't really feel anything, and if I do, I couldn't tell you what it is.' A part of the work in such cases might be to identify what each feeling is and to learn to label it, before she might even begin to learn to experience it at any depth.

The anxiety and depression linked with female problem gambling will be less likely to trigger relapse if a woman can develop strategies to avoid a cycle of overthinking problems, and getting caught in the whirlpool of additional anxiety and depression that ruminating often produces. This may feel hard at first, because worrying and being watchful may have been an unconscious coping strategy and without it she may fear leaving herself open to the worst happening. If she – as many women who gamble – is a single parent, has an overly demanding job, or has any degree of abuse in her background, she may be used to having to be in a state of high alert, and feel she is losing control if she lets go of constant worrying. Naturally, it will take practice to be able to take time off from worry. As one woman described it: 'It feels like I've taken off my armour, lying down in the middle of a battlefield, totally exposed, saying, "Here I am, come and get me!"'

If a woman is in professional support during this period, she will be supported in gradually becoming used to feeling again, after the numbing effect of gambling. As I have emphasised, an ability to tolerate a level of emotional discomfort is essential to prevent relapse. None of us can ever be certain what life will present us with, so to have some degree of tolerance for whatever is thrown our way is a part of the art of life. Some experiences in life have created emotional wounds so deep that perhaps that area will never entirely heal. If so, a woman will need to explore how to keep this particular area as protected from further pain as possible. I accept that some schools of thought might accuse me of encouraging avoidant behaviour. I see this, however, as a very positive form of avoidance, and actually more of a realistic risk assessment. Better to identify specific areas in life that prove too challenging and avoid those than continually push oneself into painful situations that are confidence destroying and, as a consequence, return to what feels like the safety and anaesthetising effects of excessive gambling and general life avoidance. Being with a level of feeling again is about balance: being with particularly troubling emotion so that a level of tolerance is learnt, but not drowning in it so that high anxiety or an unhealthy depression is triggered.

Many women describe feeling 'uncomfortable with being comfortable', because a heightened state of anxiety has become their normality. Without it, life might seem dull, flat and pointless – they experience a deadening. To prevent relapse, it is vitally important that such a woman goes forward to create a fulfilling, rewarding and interesting life. Those who leave treatment and return in six months' time having relapsed are often those for whom life has stayed the same as it was before they began to gamble. They have removed gambling, but have nothing to fill the time and space that it occupied. This is always a tricky area for many women I work with for several reasons:

- Often women have good reason through experience to fear trying new things, and so like to stay in their comfort zones.
- A woman has an association with her new routine and stability, and fears that any spontaneity or new activities may result in a return to chaos.
- Chronic health problems limit possibilities for physical activity.
- Mental health problems such as anxiety and depression may bring additional difficulties when engaging in new experiences.
- Lone parents have limited time and money to spend on themselves.
- Guilt around gambling behaviour leads to a belief that the women concerned deserve nothing for themselves.
- Guilt results in overcompensation – spending all available time and money on others.

Of all those listed, guilt is probably the most likely to trigger relapse. Feeling guilty is extremely uncomfortable and we want to get rid of the feeling as quickly as we can; for the woman in recovery, whichever way she goes about it, it could lead to gambling. Gambling to escape from feeling guilty is of course the obvious danger, but overcompensating for the consequences of past gambling behaviour and living even more rigidly by the 'Please others' rule, will sooner or later leave a woman exhausted, low, and often angry and resentful. She will be reluctant to admit that even to herself, though, because she will feel too guilty about her past gambling to acknowledge it. As a result of the pressure she puts herself under, she is more likely to bring about what she most fears – that she will let down those she cares about so deeply, because the pressure will trigger a relapse to gambling; yet again an escape trap. If she can understand this cycle, *plus* the reasons for the start of her gambling in the first place, she is more likely to be able to practice self-forgiveness and compassion, and so break free of the cycle of guilt.

We spoke earlier of the importance of routine to build a safe house, but, to move further on from gambling and not run back to it, it is important to watch for signs that the safe house built from routine is becoming a prison, in which a woman locks herself for fear of what is on the outside. Isolation and associated loneliness are primary triggers for gambling in women, and will still be there when the gambling has gone unless a woman takes steps to improve her social life. When women attend group meetings, I am careful to emphasise that the group is a space to learn confidence and skills for *how to* make friends and better relationships in general, and not the place *to* make friends. Again, with so many women having experienced a level of trauma in their lives, it is natural that they seek comfort zones, but potentially even group or one-to-one therapy could become a prison, if a woman feels she has no choice but to attend, it being her only form of social contact because she remains too afraid to seek company outside.

The benefits of group work for relapse prevention are numerous, but I would highlight:

- experiencing the healthiness and value of connecting with others;
- experiencing interdependence as positive;
- identifying skills and resources that are required for life free of gambling;
- practising social skills;
- catharsis – expression as oppose to suppression.

In order to know truly what it is she wants to bring into her life, a woman needs to know who it is she sees when she looks in the mirror – to see beyond the identity of 'gambler' and its limitations and connotations. I encourage her to ask herself questions about who she is too, beyond the identity of mother, daughter, wife, partner, her professional identity. What is it *she* wants, needs, enjoys, dislikes? What adventures might she dream of having? There may be some difficult life choices to make, perhaps because she discovers her gambling-free self is outgrowing her old life, relationships, jobs and interests. Many women describe feeling more 'grown up' as they move from the stasis of addiction that has stunted them. Managing their fears and lives better, they feel less childlike and experience a more Adult self. This in turn may have an impact on close relationships as they refuse to be limited to the role of, for example, 'Please others' or 'Be nice'. Many women embrace this change, others are unsettled by it, and a few sadly may relapse, consciously or unconsciously, to maintain the status quo, for fear of rejection of their more authentic self.

As we have discussed, fear freezes, and the fears created by gambling, and those that often created the gambling problem initially, will have meant that the woman has lost the joy in life. The ability to be spontaneous and to laugh, to rediscover creativity and playfulness is invaluable in relapse prevention. I have not yet facilitated any one group of women where at some point there have not been tears of laughter, as well as tears of sadness and frustration (and yes, at times within the same hour and a half meeting) and both kinds have been equally therapeutic if they have truly come from a woman spontaneously being her authentic, mask-free self in that moment. Not to mention of course the enormous benefits of laughter and playfulness as a release of tension and stress, and as a bonding experience with others.

Sue's story offers an example.

Sue

One woman in particular with whom I worked, and who found creativity key to her relapse prevention, was Sue. She had a background of abuse and a complex mental health diagnosis, including that of post-traumatic stress disorder. This meant that flashbacks of the abuse she had experienced would occur at any time, with unknown triggers. She suppressed all anger, because she was afraid of the power of her feelings. When either the flashbacks occurred, or she felt angry, she would severely self-harm as distraction. When she discovered the absorption of gambling online, she crossed over to that, as a coping strategy. Gambling was less physically harmful than cutting herself. The financial damage, however, left her even more anxious and depressed, and the time spent gambling meant her already limited social life began to become even more constricted.

During her time in therapy, Sue took a holiday and discovered that she enjoyed relaxing by concentrating on the glass-painting kit that she had bought as a souvenir of her holiday. She found it a welcome soothing distraction at times when she felt emotionally distressed. The absorption through focus was similar to that of online gambling, but with the benefits of expressing herself through art and feeling better after the activity, instead of worse as she did after gambling. After a time, she found that, when experiencing flashbacks or distressing emotion, she was choosing her creative activities over online gambling. I would like to note that for Sue the enjoyment of creativity and art work grew into making jewellery, and she now teaches this skill and has set up her own small business, all of which has only grown, too, her self-confidence, social life and general well-being.

Finding paths to creative self-expression for those women who find it hard to express themselves verbally is a positive release, and sometimes for all of us there may be times when we feel something at such a profound level, or in such complexity, that words cannot adequately express feeling. Drawing, writing, painting, playing music, using films or books as metaphor – all are a wonderfully rich form of self-expression. There is no 'getting it right' in producing a perfect work of art – these are a woman's *own* feelings, her *own* experiences. Expression through an art form can reverse the suppression of gambling. It offers a healthy expression and a healthy escapism. I do not know a single one of us who 'keeps it real' all the time. Escape is okay if the route is ultimately healthy, and so too the consequence. For the woman who suffers high anxiety, for example, it can be a massive relief to turn off her racing thoughts by writing something, anything, that absorbs her for a time. When she comes out of her creative bubble, she can experience a feeling of calm satisfaction at having broken the anxiety trap, but having not put herself in another trap, created, for example, by excessive gambling.

Louise Bourgeois, one of the world's leading contemporary artists found that her early childhood experiences not only inspired her work, but also that her art was a way of her expressing and coping with feelings of betrayal, anger and loneliness that had haunted her from childhood on:

> It's that anxiety is then transformed into something specific, as specific as a drawing. Then you can have access to it, you can deal with it, because it has gone from the unconscious to the conscious, which is fear. So my work is really based on the elimination of fear. (Louise Bourgeois interview with Cecelia Blomberg, 16 October, 1998. (Morris, 2007: 42, para 1)

I wish to be clear that I do not believe relapse can always be prevented, or that all situations can find resolution, via healthy expression or healthy escapism alone. Some situations require facing head on, and a very practical resolution. Relapse prevention requires that life in the real world needs to feel at the *very least* less painful than the world of excessive gambling. For the woman whose debts are unmanageable, this will be a potential trigger for relapse and seeking professional advice on this early on in treatment will be helpful. Messy and overburdened lives need to be tidied and made easier to carry. At times, in situations such as domestic violence, women may still be living day to day the fear that triggers gambling. Gambling, as we now see, is a *symptom* of underlying problems. If such underlying issues remain, the symptoms are more likely to occur all over again. Women in such situations may benefit from referral to agencies that specialise in support and advise on how to effect change.

We have spoken at length about the need for growing a stronger sense of identity beyond that of a woman who gambles, of becoming more self-aware and emotionally expressive, and developing a full and more satisfying life. Yet, the early stages of getting to this point in recovery can also be a potentially tricky time for relapse. Relapse at this stage is sometimes termed 'becoming complacent'; however, for many women who gamble, it is closely linked to a need to feel in control. Feeling stronger, her thoughts clearer, more balanced in terms of her emotions, and with an all-round greater sense of herself, a woman may be convinced that if she gambles she will be able to remain in control this time. Whether or not she is able to do so in the long term, it is impossible to say, but in early recovery it is likely that if she gambles she will *lose* control. It is how she *felt* when gambling which hooked her in initially, and the risk is that once again she will be hooked by those feelings, and gamble more time and money than she consciously intended or expected. I have worked with some women who have made a deliberate attempt at controlled gambling, because it is so important for them to feel in control of every aspect of their lives that they feel uncomfortable thinking that there is a part of themselves over which they have no control, including the part of themselves that lost control when gambling. Connected to this need to feel in control, some women fear that relapse might occur when least expected, wreaking havoc. For some, sitting with this fear of uncertainty feels intolerable and so they gamble to 'get it over with', because even knowing the worst feels easier that not knowing at all.

If and when (it is realistic to expect a 'when') relapse occurs, although painful and disruptive, recovery from it tends to be much quicker than it was when a woman originally decided to let go of gambling. She knows through experience that the anxiety and depression that are the aftermath of relapse *will* pass, and that even in a week's time she will be feeling stronger and more settled. She is therefore more likely to go through post-relapse withdrawal, resisting urges to repeat the gambling behaviour, or to cross-addict in attempts to escape her distress. Again, because she now has a frame of reference for withdrawal, she will have a 'tool kit' of strategies for distraction and self-soothing that she can draw on to ease herself through.

Chapter 11

One woman's story

If we are to truly live a life, it is inevitable that we shall experience a degree of psychological distress and emotional pain. If we cannot tolerate our emotional pain, or if when the pain is too much we cannot be supported through it, we will find a way to take flight from it. When we do so, we also leave behind so much that we might take such pleasure in. Through this book we have seen how and why problem gambling manifests. We realise that it is possible to get free of the trap it creates, and, importantly, the situational and internal traps that triggered it – that it is possible to enter the recovery process feeling like a fearful Child, and emerge with a stronger Adult self.

To pull together the key elements we have discussed in this book, let us now follow Ellen into her gambling problem and out the other side.

Ellen

Ellen was the eldest of two children and had a sister four years her junior. Her parents had both had previous failed marriages. Although both got along well with others, they had few friends outside work, and tended to keep the immediate family isolated, with the exception of visits to the extended family. Ellen remembered her mother as being emotionally distant, rarely expressing sadness, or warmth, yet often being angry. Her father was sensitive and often anxious. Her parents would often argue loudly; at these times her father would threaten to leave her mother, and this would fill Ellen with fear.

Ellen remembered there being a lot of routine in her childhood. She would be able to predict exactly what she and her family would be doing on each day of the week and described feeling a little embarrassed on Mondays at infant school, when writing her diary of the weekend, that she would only ever have the same extended family visits to report.

The routine was such that, despite their arguments, Ellen remembered feeling very secure in that her parents would always be there. She also remembered, however, what she described as feeling an unsettling sense of 'a different atmosphere' and feeling very insecure if there was any break in the routine, even in small ways such as visiting a different shopping centre with her mother at an unusual time of day.

Despite the narrowness of her world, and her parents' arguments, Ellen described an overall happy childhood, enjoying spending time engaged either alone or with her sister in fantasy games, where, in her imagination, she would travel to different lands and visit islands where imaginary playmates lived. She had a voracious appetite for reading and loved fairy tales and other stories involving elements of fantasy and magic.

In early adolescence, Ellen began to feel intolerant of the rigid family routine. She would often think her parents unfairly strict and controlling in wanting her to return home earlier than her friends, or not allowing her to leave the town they lived in to take shopping trips with friends. Arguments with her parents would often develop when she would angrily shout that she would never get married and end up like them.

At school, Ellen always worked hard, was well behaved and received good reports, but often found she was too distracted by social relationships and a developing interest in romance with boys to focus on homework. She did well enough in her final exams to attend college and took A levels, intending to go on to study for a law degree at university.

When 19 years old, Ellen met the man who was soon to be her husband. She had had a few boyfriends before that time, and found that she very quickly became emotionally attached and anxious about those relationships. When she met Paul, it proved the same, and she was pleased that he was in a hurry for them to marry because she felt this brought her a sense of the security and stability she craved.

Ellen and Paul married within a year of meeting, and Ellen became pregnant with their first child almost immediately. This meant giving up her university place, but she was delighted at the prospect of becoming a mother and having a family. When their son was born, Ellen settled easily into the role of wife and mother, and took pleasure in running the home and looking after her family.

When their daughter was 6 months old, the couple moved to a larger home and Ellen noticed herself feeling depressed. She began to question how it might be if this were to be her life from now on. She and her husband began to argue frequently. After these arguments, Ellen would be upset and fearful that her husband would leave her.

Two years after their first child was born, Ellen became pregnant again. Her husband was unhappy and unsure he wanted another child, but he encouraged Ellen to go through with the pregnancy. Three days after their second child was born, her husband who had been cold and distant throughout her pregnancy told Ellen he was leaving her for someone else. Ellen felt completely devastated, reeling from shock, and as though her whole world had been shaken apart. The next morning, in acute psychological, emotional and still physical pain, she found herself tempted to take the painkillers she had brought home from hospital with a bottle of whisky, because she could not imagine ever feeling any better than she did in that moment.

Family and friends were supportive, but Ellen could remember very little about the first six months after her husband left. She described being on autopilot regarding her care for the children, feeling indescribable sadness, terrified of the world, intensely lonely and disorientated.

It was around seven months after the separation that a friend suggested that she and Ellen might go out for an evening. Ellen felt a sense of fear and emptiness as they visited local pubs. While her friend was at the bar, Ellen began to play a slot machine and found that it lowered her anxiety. She won a little money too, which lifted her mood.

After that evening, Ellen found that she thought about the slot machine a lot and she got a babysitter so that she could visit the amusement arcade with another friend. She enjoyed the way she could forget about her problems and being 'mum' for a time. When she returned home, she would feel better about her responsibilities and a happier and more engaged mother. Life on benefits meant money was always short, and, as with everything else, Ellen budgeted carefully for her gambling time. She found, however, that it was increasingly hard to stop playing, and began to notice that she only felt okay when in the arcade. She also found that, when she lost money, she would panic and try to win it back. When she started to lose more than she could afford, she tried to stop, but without gambling felt so depressed that she would struggle to get up and function. Despite her feelings and situation, she was determined to be a good mother to her children.

Ellen remembered her lowest point as having barely enough money to eat for the week, let alone pay bills or a babysitter. That night, she waited until her children were asleep in bed, then crept out of the house to go to the arcade. She said she felt sick with terror that they might wake up and discover her gone, or that someone else might discover she had left them alone, and yet her craving for gambling was so great that it felt as if she had no choice: she could not face another evening alone with the misery of what her life had become.

Five years after she began gambling, Ellen returned to education and completed a law degree. She found that studying helped her to limit her gambling, although she entered a phase of acute panic attacks where she would fear she was having a heart attack and make regular A&E visits. Her GP suggested she take antidepressants, but this bemused Ellen who felt insulted, believing she was not depressed. She again began to gamble more frequently and fell into debt. Behind the professional persona, which was efficient and positive, her life was chaotic, and she was often highly anxious.

When her youngest child was 7 years old, Ellen met a man she was to marry two years later. He was dependable and kind and, although she did not feel excited by the relationship, she felt she was making a good decision for herself and her children. At first she enjoyed the sense of stability the relationship brought and made a conscious decision to stop gambling. She read self-help books on the subject and managed to control her behaviour. However, a year later she found herself feeling low and bored, and began to gamble again. Her marriage and the routine of home life felt increasingly oppressive; she became depressed and irritable and she and her husband began to argue. Ellen found herself pushing her husband away, and yet at the same time feeling terrified it might work and he would leave. Her gambling continued through the remaining two years of their marriage, and, despite her husband's suspicions around where money was going, and where Ellen was going when she was often absent, she kept it hidden by weaving elaborate tales.

After three years, the marriage ended and Ellen felt a mixture of relief and excitement at the chance of a new start, and anxiety and emptiness at the blank canvas of life before her. She discovered online bingo and once again her gambling escalated, and to greater proportions than before. All the promises she had made to herself about the fresh start were dissolved, along with the sum of money from her divorce. She found that her alcohol intake increased too, because she would use drinking to drown her thoughts and feelings about the debt and chaos her gambling was bringing about, including the new phase of panic attacks she had entered.

Fourteen years after Ellen began to gamble, she had a good career and was respected and liked at work. In her personal life, however, she was lonely; her children had lives of their own and spent more time out of the home. She had no partner and did not share her true feelings with her few close friends, who saw her as strong and capable and always positive. Large and increasing debts meant that she was finding it harder to manage. Her gambling was as she described it 'wild', and left her feeling desperately low, 'unclean' and dissatisfied. It no longer made her happy; she no longer wanted to engage in the behaviour, and yet still felt compelled to. It was on one weekend, alone, after her youngest son had told her he intended to move out to live with friends, that Ellen finally hit rock bottom. With no money to gamble, or buy alcohol, she finally felt the full impact of her miserable situation and feared a complete breakdown. She found herself once more with suicidal thoughts. She made a decision to seek treatment.

When Ellen arrived at her first therapy session, she was well dressed, poised and smiling. She was quick to tell me that she knew what her problem was, that she was in debt because she had been gambling too much, for too long, and that she was now trying to win her money back and just losing more. She knew this was stupid, because everyone knows you can never win your money back, especially from machines, yet she could not help but hang on to that thought that maybe one more go could make that change. 'To walk away, when you just never know,' Ellen felt intolerable. She had to stay and play one more reel. Just in case. She said she knew that did not make sense either because, if she did win her money back, she would not leave with it – she would stay and play more. The worst thing of all would be if someone else came along and put in £5 and won all she had put in. She had seen that happen: others stand and watch a person play, waiting for them to leave so they can take their machine. That was 'sickening', as she described it.

Ellen described her online gambling as 'like another world'. She liked being in complete isolation, but at the same time felt she had friends among the other players. She would play both fruit machines or online for such long periods that she could hear the sounds of the machines ringing in her head for hours afterwards. Or she would feel confused and disembodied after playing online.

I asked Ellen when she had started to gamble. She told me in matter-of-fact tones about her husband leaving, and the depression, but that was years ago, and she was over all that now; she felt nothing about it, except bad that her children had missed out on family life. When I asked about her early life, she told me everything had been 'great', that she had had a perfect family. Anyway, that was years ago, too. What she was concerned about now was stopping gambling.

I asked Ellen what she wanted to get from the process of therapy. 'Just to stop gambling,' she replied. 'It's insane, and it's messing up my life, and on paper I have a good life. And I should be happy.'

We ended the first session with my saying that we could work together to work out how gambling made sense to her. And that life may *look* good on paper, but that it might be valuable to look at whether it *felt* good to her.

We can see how in that first session Ellen was keen to stay in control. Despite the moment of despair that brought her to crisis and into therapy, she had quickly regrouped. One way of her remaining in control was to stay talking about the safe topic of gambling behaviour. It was the thing I already knew about her, so she could keep herself safe while she worked out whether she could trust me, and the process of therapy. She saw her only problem as the gambling behaviour, either because she was genuinely unaware of the causal factors, or because she feared revealing them and opening up a box of horrors she was not prepared to deal with. Gambling had been helping her to keep the lid tightly shut. Talking about the gambling problem was a way of her escaping from the pressure of the session, because it was an escape mechanism in her life outside.

Ellen was no longer in denial of her gambling problem, but in denial of the effect of the break-up of her first marriage. She described remembering little about the first six months at that time, so indicating it was perhaps a genuine trauma. After trauma, we often block out elements of the event that we unconsciously deem too difficult to experience. Ellen also did not see any value in talking about her early life and seeing it through childlike eyes as 'all good'. Already we see the impact of her early life, of the family keeping themselves to themselves, and her earlier way of behaving at school is still apparent when, despite her dire situation, she presents herself to me as smiling and pleasant – we see 'Please others'. Her mother's cool and emotionally distant behaviour we hear from Ellen's story, and see in her relating with me as both 'Don't be close' and 'Be strong'. 'Be strong' had manifested in her refusing the GP's diagnosis of depression and offer of medication, because she felt they implied weakness.

For the first three or four sessions, Ellen remained focused on talk of her gambling behaviour and kept a sense of her professional self to the fore while relating to me. This part of her was able to cope well and she felt strong presenting herself in this way. By this stage she had already managed to stay gambling free, and was feeling an enormous sense of relief that her anxiety was reduced and her preoccupation was lessening, so she was able to concentrate on work projects and regain some order in life.

When she arrived for session 14, we were in a different consulting room from the one we had used previously. Ellen seemed unsettled by this and expressed feeling strange to be in a different place, not to have 'her' chair, and to have broken our routine. We spoke about that fact that gambling, from the outside, appeared to be all about chaos, but in fact was quite predictable in terms of both the behaviour and consequences: that most women knew how they would feel during and afterwards. We were later to identify that this made gambling more appealing to Ellen than drugs or alcohol, because she initially felt in control of her experience of escapism. It was only when gambling created higher anxiety that she then turned to alcohol in an attempt to control those feelings too. I commented on how I remembered Ellen speaking of her childhood and how predictable it was, how she had spoken of the uncomfortable sense of 'a different atmosphere' if anything changed, as had our room that day.

We spent a lot of that session exploring how Ellen had grown up with an ambivalent relationship to routine and ritual. There had been so much of it in childhood that she only felt safe and comfortable with the predictable. Both her parents encouraged a fearful view of the world outside the family, and subsequently Ellen had recorded a 'Be careful' rule. At the same time, she felt deadened and trapped by predictability. As a child, she had found ways to escape it by creating a fantasy world to disappear into, or in the absorption of voracious reading. We identified that her marriages reflected how she had felt in childhood: at once craving the security and stability of knowing what would happen each and every day, but feeling suffocated, resentful and trapped. Not wanting to get married and end up like her parents, but at the same time feeling the terror she had felt as a child at her father's threats of abandonment, if she imagined her husband leaving. What she had screamed at her parents – that she would not end up like them – she had ended up screaming inside, and, when the screams got too loud in her second marriage, gagging herself with gambling. In reality, gambling had been an extension of that early escapist behaviour.

Eighteen sessions into therapy, Ellen had formed a strong working relationship with me, and was beginning to let go of some of her need to be in control. She was noticing that, as she gained more and more gambling-free time, she was beginning to experience her feelings more. Although still appreciating the benefits of being less anxious, she described her mood as flat. In one session, she reported seeing an empty life stretching ahead of her, and that she imagined always needing to remain conscious that she might be tempted to gamble to lift her mood. Although her debts were under control, and there were no urgent problems in the here and now, she was finding it difficult to keep her own company. She disclosed that she had had urges to gamble again, and that one evening she had found herself playing for a couple of hours on an online gambling site. I asked her if there had been anything in particular going on for her at that time. She said that she had been looking at photographs of herself, and her first son. She had remembered how she had left her children alone to go to the arcade, and how even when she was with them she felt she was like a ghost in their lives, because she was too preoccupied with gambling, or too miserable and anxious from the consequences of it, to be truly present. She described to me the deep level of shame and guilt she felt at her behaviour, how she hated herself, and imagined I was disgusted with her.

We can see how for Ellen the further she moved away from problem gambling behaviour, the nearer she came to experiencing her true feelings, and along with them the guilt and regret for the lost time and damaged relationships. Her children had grown, but she had not been around or present enough to truly witness or take part in that, because she was disconnected by gambling. It was these thoughts and feelings that had triggered a relapse.

Ellen continued to feel she deserved to be punished for her treatment of her children, and went through a phase of relapse, which only compounded her negative self-image. She adhered rigidly to the rules for life her mother had given her, and withheld warmth from herself, so increasing the urges to gamble. Despite her improving environment, she was creating a world within herself that felt a intolerable place to inhabit.

In one session, Ellen again mentioned the photographs of herself and her children, and I asked what she saw when she looked at herself, the person she had been back then, before her marriage broke down. She was silent, then became tearful, struggling to say that she thought how young and naïve she looked and then, speaking of her then husband leaving her, quietly said, 'What a horrible thing to happen to someone.' She spent the rest of the session sobbing, and grieving for the young woman she had been, abandoned and terrified, and feeling so alone. She was in a new and deep level of psychological and emotional pain as she began to experience the feelings that had been blocked out first by the trauma of her experience, and then by gambling. She allowed herself to understand that her gambling had been a way of her trying to survive. She told me how she felt that she had been wrenched out of the world she had loved, of family and security; that suddenly, it had been snatched away from her. That she felt a physical pain in her stomach if ever she thought of it, and felt sick with emotion, similar to the 'sickening' feeling she described experiencing in the arcade at the thought of someone else coming along and taking away the money she had put into the fruit machine – one loss reflecting another.

We explored Ellen's suicidal thoughts as being brought about by sheer terror at imagining life in an unfamiliar and lonely world; that, despite being mother, she was back in her Child self, who had felt unsettled by even the smallest break in routine; that later on this high level of anxiety and overwhelming responsibility had manifested itself in panic attacks. She was experiencing her childhood fear of abandonment.

From that point, Ellen began to forgive herself through her understanding of the *reasons* for and *meaning* of her gambling. As a result, she allowed herself to learn self-soothing techniques, and to work on relapse prevention. We explored her rules of 'Be strong' and 'Please others', and how they had worked against her as they drove suppression of her feelings and kept her psychologically and emotionally distant from others, and we discussed the potential support that close relationship offers. We also identified that Ellen was ragingly angry with her children's father for his treatment of her and her children. We explored how, because she had witnessed her volatile parents' arguments, she had learnt to fear her own anger. She had suppressed this too, by gambling.

During Ellen's 24 sessions of therapy, she learnt to identify the triggers for her gambling and to soothe herself through uncomfortable thoughts and feelings that were the triggers for her gambling. She learnt to like and respect herself again. She understood how gambling had made sense to her at the time, because it had helped her to survive a traumatic episode in her life. She worked through the painful stage of guilt, remorse and regret; grieving for lost money, time and opportunities. Through this process, life gradually became less about survival and more about experiencing and living.

At a one-year follow-up appointment, Ellen had remained gambling free. She still had times when she missed the escapism offered by gambling. Like the fairy stories she had loved as a child, gambling offered her a transcendent quality. Online gambling even offered imaginary friends, in the form of the virtual friends she met online. There were still times when the 'real world' felt a little too much, or, conversely, just not enough. Through working on how to better tolerate uncertainty, however, Ellen now knows not to put herself into traps as a way to ease her anxiety around the unpredictable. She is learning how to balance her needs for security and stability with her need for adventure and living a full life.

Chapter 12

Reflections on practice

I thank you, reader, for your attention, and hope I have managed to convey a greater understanding of the woman who falls into the trap of excessive gambling. We have seen how it is about so much more than the money: at its very core, it is about society – its values, morals, pressures and lack of support. It is about families and partners – problems created either by the not having them, or the having them. It is about interpersonal relationships and how these create the dynamics of the relationship we have with ourselves.

The recovery process, the healing, the treatment – whatever and however we wish to term it – is in reversing the destructive process of negative relationship with others and the self. It is in initially finding support, encouragement and understanding in relationship with at least one other, to enable the identification, and replacement, of whatever it is that a woman has felt her relationship with gambling has provided; and for her to re-enter the world with a more expansive life view, including trusting in supportive others, but also in herself, with a strong Adult self, capable of making healthier life choices, capable of keeping herself safe, but at the same time continually evolving and engaged with living a life, as opposed to remaining in the stasis of a grey existence. The recovery process includes her developing ways of expressing rather than suppressing troubling thoughts and feelings. It requires practical adjustments to whatever it is that has triggered the need to escape through gambling.

Buried beneath layers of addiction and psychological and emotional suppression have frequently been found some of the warmest, most creative, resilient women. I am aware that the tone of this book is one of warmth and often pride in the women I have met. It is, too, an unapologetic tone, because over the years I have worked with so many women, absolutely determined despite all obstacles to stand and face, take responsibility for and change their desperate situation. Although much of this book is anecdotal, my respect for their strength is evidence based. My practice has often given me reason not only to feel a sense of pride in the women I see transforming themselves and their lives, but also profound pride in what it is to be a woman.

I have been asked the questions, 'How does my work affect me? Do I not go away burdened with the painful stories?' I answer that, in the therapy room, I *feel with* the woman who is telling her story as she experiences her pain. I hope to always do so. As Yalom put it in his book, *The Gift of Therapy*, men of steel are robots (Yalom, 2002: 14). I feel hopeful that he would not mind my extending this theory to women too. I think the day that I become a robot is the day I would need to cease practice. Our feelings are perhaps the lubricant that stops us as professionals from rusting and eventually seizing up. How can I encourage someone to tolerate her own feelings if I have become desensitised to my own? What helps me not to leave carrying them home with me is, I believe, what helps the woman I am working with to remain gambling free: having a full and varied life, with supportive family and friends; these give balance to my life.

For the reader interested in practising problem gambling therapy with women, or who is engaged in any form of regular support with women letting go of excessive gambling, I have compiled below hints for practice to cover issues raised when I am supervising or delivering training to other clinicians:

- Live a life. It is so easy to get bogged down in theory and research and technique, and to forget that modelling a way of being is a key element of the therapeutic process. Remember that in all likelihood we are working with someone who has been disengaged from life and relationships through their gambling problem. A 'Don't do as I do, do as I say' professional will be spotted, and will not inspire confidence in the same way as the one who has a go at being out in the world themselves. So, live a full and varied life; maybe let life get messy now and then; love, be hurt; try new things that create anxiety; be joyful, be human... It will all enrich personal life and professional work, and, to work in the way this book describes, the two are inseparable. Remember to take a few healthy risks (this is different from being reckless) because, as we have explored, this is something the women who gambles finds so hard to do, and what her gambling problem is *not* about. The risk to her is in living her life.
- Develop a continual curiosity and understanding of personal attitudes towards the kind of issues we have discussed as being common

themes of the work: abandonment, anger, anxiety, loneliness, loss, rejection, sadness. The better we know ourselves and our own attitudes towards issues we are working with, the better we are able to be alongside another while they discover their own relationship to these experiences; the less likely we are to be lost along with them in a fog of confusion and fear.

• Whatever the clinical setting or profession, access to regular supervision and/or debriefing is essential. Often, we are honoured with being trusted with stories of pain, sadness and trauma, and it is important to have support for processing how it is to be witness to these.

• Work in areas outside the field of problem gambling, and/or develop other interests outside the world of work. It may be tempting not to, because working in this area can be so very satisfying and rewarding. If working in this field exclusively, watch out for signs of any developing 'factory system' mentality. An indication of this is work feeling stale, or developing a too formulaic way of working with 'female gamblers', rather than women who are gambling problematically. There is a subtle difference, and that is in whether we are focusing on just behavioural change, as the first description might imply, or working with a whole woman in order to effect behavioural change. If we are working with a whole woman and remain curious about who she is and why she is gambling, the work is endlessly interesting and fresh in my view, despite regular themes to problem gambling behaviour and treatment.

• Have personal relationships of all kinds: friends, family, romance, colleagues, pets. Working at the degree of engagement we have discussed in this book, it may be tempting to feel that at the end of a working day the need for emotional and psychological intimacy has been satisfied. It has not. We have been present and connected, and a real self in that time, *for our client*, but we have not truly met our own needs for being seen, heard or even physically held. The danger lies hidden that – as with gambling – the therapeutic work in itself becomes addictive; that, because of the quality of relational work, it may take the edge off the need to relate with others in our world outside the professional setting. Just like gambling has taking the edge off the hunger for closeness for many women. It may be easy at times to forget that we have personal needs, because yet again, as with excessive gambling, working in this relational way can *feel* as though emotional needs are being met, without the complicated business of personal relationships that require us to reveal more of our whole self. If tiredness creeps in and relationships outside work are tricky, to go home, shut the door and relate as remotely as possible, maybe just send a text or posting something on Facebook feels tempting. There are similarities in the bubble created by excessive gambling and the bubble of isolation, which, if we are unaware, can be created by *working* with problem gambling, I hope make sense.

- The landscape of the gambling industry rapidly changes shape. It never hurts to keep up with developments. My experience is that it is unnecessary to understand exactly how to play any, or every, form of gambling. What is valuable is to understand what the psychological and emotional gain from each mode of gambling is for each woman. There are, as we have seen, patterns to this, such as the absorption of slot machine playing and online gambling, the 'buzz' that might be gained from horse racing. Much more valuable for the therapeutic work, however, than our precise understanding of the mechanics of how to place a bet, play a slot machine or a hand of poker is encouraging the woman with the problem to explore and therefore to understand . . . what it is that she herself gets from the gambling experience.

- Be prepared, if working in this field and asked what it is that you do, after giving your answer, to then explain the entire psychology of women and problem gambling, within a couple of minutes . . . Most people are fascinated by – but do not understand – problem gambling. Almost always my experience has been that they are still genuinely surprised that *women* have gambling problems. Although offered as light-hearted observation and advice to professionals, this experience leaves me mindful of the difficulties facing women should they choose to disclose their gambling problem to another person. They are still often risking lack of understanding, shock and disapproval.

- Be prepared that the woman you are working with might ask whether you have ever tried gambling, or engaged in it as a regular pastime. My experience in supervision and clinical training is that this question often throws clinicians more than any other ostensibly more probing request for self-disclosure. Clinicians often feel as if they are being 'tested' according to their answer. Some might choose not to answer, but I wonder what is to be gained by this stance, and believe it can have a negative impact on the work. This is especially so if one is working with a woman whose experience leaves her finding it difficult to trust; she may often mistrust the professional's motives in lack of transparency. For the practitioner who gambles, either recreationally, or in the past problematically, whether to make a personal disclosure and answer 'yes', whether to decline to answer at all, might depend on personal attitudes to gambling. If gambling itself is the cause of problems, there may be less inclination to say 'yes', fearing being seen as hypocritical. If gambling is seen as a form of entertainment and escapism, which as with any form of escapism can get out of hand and become a symptom of life difficulties, it might feel more comfortable to say 'yes'. I find that women with a gambling problem ask this question less often than men. The reason for this is that, because they frequently gamble for escape and absorption and so choose forms of gambling that require low skill levels, they are less concerned about understanding the mechanics of gambling behaviour, and therefore, too, about whether the professional understands them either. Women are more concerned about the underlying and accompanying issues. If a woman does ask the question, the subtext is often whether she will be understood and accepted without judgement. Will she shock the professional if she discloses the irrational drives she experiences and the lengths she has gone to as a consequence of gambling?

• The following quote by Sue Perkins is from an article in which she is talking of her joy at finding that piano playing was not just all about being bound by technique: 'Yes technique is important, but only in so far as it gives you a place from which to express yourself. Music is about inhabiting the moment. Absolutely. Completely' (Perkins, 2012: 9). As professionals working with problem gambling, of course we need technique and a framework, particularly so when one of the consequences of gambling is inner and outer chaos. If within that framework, however, as with piano playing, there can be a degree of expression of the professional's authentic self, developing an individual style of practice will not only be an incredibly satisfying way to practise, but it will also encourage the woman letting go of gambling to be her authentic self, too; at first, just there in that moment; absolutely; completely; eventually, in her world outside the professional setting; encouraging her to outgrow the narrow, restrictive world of problem gambling.

I would like to close with hearing the voices of some of the woman with whom I have worked, as they reflect on life, now free of problem gambling:

I have learnt to be myself and that it's okay to say 'no' occasionally.

[The] group has taught me that I cannot go through life alone and more importantly I don't want to. It has taught me to trust other people, which I did find very hard.

This group will end but our lives will just begin. With the strength and courage from the group we have known, we can all face another day in this world.

I am excited by life and eager to live it. I cannot wait to see what is around the corner and make choices and decisions integral to my needs.

I'm not going back to that dark place where I lied and cheated friends, as long as I am drawing breath. It's great to be alive.

Referral organisations

For those curious to find out more, wishing to seek support or to make a referral.

Citizens Advice Bureau (CAB)

http://www.citizensadvice.co.uk

Community Action for Responsible Gambling (CARG)

Addressing problem gambling issues in the community.
http://www.carg.co.uk
T: 020 7235 2768

Consumer Credit Counselling Service (CCCS)

Free online debt advice.
http://www.cccs.co.uk
Helpline: 0800 138 1111

Couple Connection

Free relationship advice and support, helping couples, families and parents deal with relationship problems.
http://www.the coupleconnection.net

European Association for the Study of Gambling (EASG)

Provides a forum for the systematic study, discussion and dissemination of knowledge about all matters relating to the study of gambling in Europe
http://www.easg.org

Family Lives

National charity providing help and support in all aspects of family life.
http://www.familylives.org.uk
Helpline: 0808 800 2222

Gam-Anon

A fellowship of men and women who are husbands, wives, partners, family and friends, affected by someone who has a gambling problem. Offering group support and help.
http://www.gamanon.org.uk

Gamble Aware

Aiming to promote responsible gambling.
http://www.gambleaware.co.uk
T: 020 7287 1994

Gamblers Anonymous

A fellowship of men and women who have a gambling problem. Offering group support and help.
http://www.gamblersanonymous.org.uk

Gambling Commission

Regulating commercial gambling in Great Britain.
http://www.gamblingcommission.gov.uk
T: 0121 230 6666

GamCare

Support, information and advice to anyone suffering from a gambling problem.
http://www.gamcare.org.uk
Helpline: 0808 8020 133

Gordon Moody Association

Specialist support and treatment for acutely addicted gamblers.
http://www.gordonmoody.org.uk
T: 01384 241 292

Level Ground Therapy

Specialist support and treatment for women with a gambling problem.
http://www.levelgroundtherapy.com
T: 0845 2666 658

Mind

Advice and support for anyone with a mental health problem.
http://www.mind.org.uk
T: 0300 123 3393

Money Advice Service

Free, independent financial advice.
http://www.moneyadviceservice.org.uk
T: 0300 500 5000

National Problem Gambling Clinic

Treating problem gamblers, their partners and family members in England and Wales.
http://www.cnwl.nhs.uk
T: 020 7534 6699

Platform 51

Formerly YWCA, a charity that supports girls and women and promotes equality.
http://www.platform51.org
T: 01865 304200

Refuge

Help for women and children who have experienced domestic violence.
http://www.refuge.org.uk
Helpline: 0808 2000 247

Relate

Offers relationship counselling, sex therapy, workshops, mediation, consultations and support. Face to face, by telephone and online.
http://www.relate.org.uk
T: 0300 100 1234

Responsible Gambling Trust (RGT)

Aiming to minimise problem gambling and gambling-related harm in British society through research, education and treatment.
http://www.responsiblegamblingtrust.org.uk
T: 020 7287 1994

Samaritans

Confidential emotional support 24/7.
http://www.samaritans.org
Helpline: 0845 7909 090

Society for the Study of Gambling

Research group and forum concerned with the studying of gambling and associated issues.
http://www.societystudygambling.co.uk
T: 020 7242 5905

References

American Heritage Medical Dictionary (2007) Boston, MA: Houghton Mifflin.

American Psychiatric Association (2000) *Diagnostic and Statistical Manual of Mental Disorders (DSM) Problem Gambling Screen.* Washington DC: American Psychiatric Association.

American Psychiatric Association (2005) *Diagnostic and Statistical Manual of Mental Disorders, (DSM-IV),* 4th edition. Washington DC: American Psychiatric Association.

BBC (1994) 'On this Day', http://news.bbc.co.uk/onthisday/hi/dates/stories/november/19/newsid_3702000/3702998.stm, accessed November 2012.

Beck, A.T. and Emery, G. (1985) *Anxiety Disorders and Phobias. A Cognitive Perspective.* New York: Basic Books.

Berne, E. (2010) *The Games People Play.* London: Penguin.

Bradford Cannon, W. (1915) *Bodily Changes in Pain, Hunger, Fear and Rage: An Account of Recent Researches into the Function of Emotional Excitement.* Appleton-Century-Crofts.

Briere, J. (1992) *Child Abuse Trauma.* London: Sage.

de Botton, A. (2000) *The Consolations of Philosophy.* London: Penguin Books.

Caernarfon Denbigh Herald (2011) 'Fifteen Per Cent Increase in UK Women Suffering from Gambling Addiction', http://www.caernarfonherald.co.uk/caernarfon-county-news/special-features/2011/07/26/fifteen-per-cent-increase-in-uk-women-suffering-from-gambling-addiction-88817-29121478, accessed November 2012.

CAIN Web Service (n.d.) 'Chapter 12 from *The Price of My Soul* by Bernadette Devlin (1969)', http://www.Cain.ulst.ac.uk/events/crights/devlin69.htm, accessed July 2012.

Cameron, J. (1993) *The Artist's Way.* London: Pan Books.

Coleridge, M.E. (1896) 'The Other Side of a Mirror', http://classiclit.about.com/library/bl-etexts/mecoleridge/bl-mecoleridge-otherside.htm, accessed July 2012.

Curtis, V. (2002) *Virginia Woolfe's Women.* London: Hale.

Drucker Institute (2012) 'The Risk One Cannot Afford to Take', http://thedx.druckerinstitute.com/2012/05/the-risk-one-cannot-afford, accessed July 2012).

eCogra (2010) 'World's Largest Study of the Online Gambler Revealed', http://www.ecogra.org/pressroom/pressreleases/pressreleasesview.aspx?id=fcc3ea a2-48cc-4240-b8a4-a48132656ee4, accessed November 2012.

Estés, C. (1992) *Women Who Run With the Wolves*. London: Rider.

Gambling Commission (2005) 'Gambling Act 2005', http://www.gambling commission.gov.uk/licensing_compliance__enfo/gambling_related_legislati on.aspx, accessed November 2012.

Gambling Commission (2010) 'British Gambling Prevalence Survey 2010', http://www.gamblingcommission.gov.uk/research__consultations/gambling_ research/british_gambling_prevalence_su/bgps_2010.aspx, accessed November 2012.

Gilbert, E. (2006) *Eat, Pray, Love*. London: Bloomsbury.

Harding, M. (1967) *The Way of All Women*. London: Rider.

Kirschenbaum, H. and Land Henderson V. (eds) (2001) *The Carl Rogers Reader*. London: Constable.

Lawton, G. (2011) 'Evolutionary Guru: Don't Believe Everything you Think', http://www.newscientist.com/article/mg21128335300-evolutionary-guru-don't-believe-everything-you-think-.html?full=true, accessed June 2012.

Lips, H. (2006) *A New Psychology Of Women*. New York: McGraw-Hill.

MailOnline (2011) 'Successful and Childless: The Career Women from Generation X who Have it all ... Except a Family', http://www.daily mail.co.uk/femail/article-2005556/Successful-childless-The-career-women-Generation-X—family.html, accessed November 2012.

Morris, F. (ed.) (2007) *Louise Bourgeois*. London: Tate.

National Lottery (2012) 'Homepage', http://www.nationallottery.co.uk/player/p/home.ftl, accessed June 2012.

Nguyen, T. (2011) 'An Introduction to Gambling Addiction', http://www.gamblinghelper.com/gambling_addiction/page/an_introduction_to_gambling_addiction,accessed June 2012.

Orriss, M. (2004) 'The Karpman Drama Triangle', http://www.coaching supervisionacademy.com/thought-leadership/the-karpman-drama-triangle, accessed July 2012.

Perkins, S. (2012) 'If at First You . . .', London: *Radio Times*, p. 9.

Platform 51 (2011) 'Antidepressants', http://www.platform51.org/whatwedo/antidepressants, accessed June 2012).

Roethke, T. (1957) 'Infirmity', http://www.poemhunter.com/poem/infirmity, accessed July 2012.

Rogers, C.R. (2000) *Client Centered Therapy*. London: Constable.

Rollnick, S. and Miller, M.R. (1995) 'Motivational Interviewing, Clinical Issues', http://www.motivationalinterview.net/clinical/whatismi.html, accessed November 2012.

Thomas, N. (2012) 'Young Players Behind 8pc Rise in Rank Profits', http://www.telegraph.co.uk/finance/newsbysector/retailandconsumer/leisure/9073053/Young-bingo-players-behind-8pc-rise-in-Rank-profits.html, accessed November 2012.

Wilson, J. (2011) 'Equality and Human Rights Impact Assessment (EIA) Preliminary Screening Template', http://www.plymouthpct.nhs.uk/Corporate Information/policiesprocedures/Documents/Equality%20Impact%20Assessm ents/2011%20-/EIA%20isolation.pdf, accessed November 2012).

Wood, Z. (2011) 'Asda Warns of Frail Consumer Confidence as Shoppers Spend Less', http://www.guardian.co.uk/business/2011/feb/22/asda-consumer-spending-supermarkets, accessed June 2012.

Woodman, M (1982) *Addiction to Perfection*. Toronto: Inner City Books.

Yale School of Medicine (2012) 'Women's Health Research at Yale. Gambling', http://medicine.yale.edu/whr/partnerships/cores/addictive/types/index.aspx# page3, accessed November 2012.

Yalom, I.D. (2002) *The Gift of Therapy*. London: Piatkus.

Index